LIFT
AS I CLIMB

An Immigrant Girl's Journey
Through Corporate America

JACKIE GLENN

authorHOUSE®

AuthorHouse™
1663 Liberty Drive
Bloomington, IN 47403
www.authorhouse.com
Phone: 1 (800) 839-8640

Scripture taken from The Holy Bible, King James Version. Public Domain

Scripture quotations marked NIV are taken from the Holy Bible, New
International Version®. NIV®. Copyright © 1973, 1978, 1984 by International
Bible Society. Used by permission of Zondervan. All rights reserved. [Biblica]

Published by AuthorHouse 03/12/2019

ISBN: 978-1-7283-0301-7 (sc)
ISBN: 978-1-7283-0302-4 (hc)
ISBN: 978-1-7283-0315-4 (e)

Library of Congress Control Number: 2019902637

Print information available on the last page.

This book is printed on acid-free paper.

CONTENTS

DEDICATION

It gives me great joy to dedicate this book to my dear mom, Christianna Sterling. Although you have been gone for almost twenty years, I miss you dearly, as if you only left me yesterday. You were the quintessential supermom with your eleven children. You always instilled in us that we could do anything we set out to do. Your drive, courage, resilience, integrity and all-around positive view on life were all gifts that I inherited. On days when I think that something is too hard, or when I get super nervous and worried, I think of you and what you would say: "Perseverance my child." Mom, I love you and I know that you are in heaven looking down at me. There are not enough words to express how much your influence has steered my life and career. Love you always.

To my brother Ken, your departure from this earth was unexpected and I miss you a ton. Your jovial personality would light up any room. To my dear sister Beverly, you also left us too soon. Dedicating this book to you both reminds me of how precarious life can be and that tomorrow isn't promised to us. In your honor, I am determined to live life to the fullest.

Windsor Glenn, my husband of 35 years, you are my ride or die, the nut to my bolt, the cream to my coffee and you are always my biggest cheerleader. Even when self-doubt arises in me, your love and support are always present. You complete me and to you I also dedicate this book.

To my children, Nicole, Alicia and Wayne, as offspring of immigrant parents you wear that distinction so proudly. You are always curious to learn and experience your roots and that is a blessing within itself. Love you all to the moon and back.

FOREWORD

You are going to LOVE this book! If it reinforces life principles that you have already begun to practice, you will be shifted to an even higher level of thinking. If it is your first step into the journey of self-awareness and elevation, the vision is clearly laid out with the ten gems that Jackie Glenn so brilliantly presents.

Lift as I Climb ~ An Immigrant Girl's Journey Through Corporate America is a powerful testament of what happens when you move through the world with personal strength, resilience and boldness. It also shows the unexpected blessings that are returned to you when you lift others with faith, integrity and empathy.

Jackie's journey to America as an immigrant at the age of 20 is inspiring. The courage it must have taken to leave her family and move to a foreign country with nothing in search of a better life is breathtaking! Her ability to adapt, survive and succeed in a country where the color of her skin added to her already insurmountable challenges is truly remarkable. Jackie's journey prepared her to tell the story in a way that delivers meaning to those who care and instruction to those who want to learn. Because she was raised in another country and has extensive professional international experience, her expertise is authentic.

Having known Jackie for over 30 years, I can speak from personal experience about her gift for lifting others. She has always been the best friend who is non-judgmental. She was the 'extra parent' that I needed when I was going through a divorce with two small children – even though she had her own husband and small children. She introduced me to the career that has changed my life!

This book is necessary. It is currently a critical topic written by an expert about things that people are genuinely interested in as women become more influential to the world. Use this book and her gems to find your own gems.

Gloria Mayfield Banks
Independent Elite Executive National Sales Director
#1 Mary Kay, Inc., North America
International Speaker and Success Strategist

ACKNOWLEDGEMENTS

---◆---

This book is one of my proudest and most challenging accomplishments. I would not have seen it to completion without a few individuals who have dedicated their resources, time and effort in ensuring that I stayed the course.

I want to first thank my sister, Dr. Sandra Bailey, who pushed and prodded me beyond measure. She believed in me when I did not believe in myself. Your expertise and insights as a four time published author has made the process so much easier. Thanks for the long hours, your insight, attention to details and patience you have invested in this project. There is no doubt in my mind that this book would not have become a reality without your love and strong support.

Special thanks to Dr. Larthenia Howard, author of *How To Write A Book In 31 Days*. In my case, a bit longer! What started out as business helped me gain a sister. Even when the contracted portion of your work was completed, your weekly check-ins and encouragement helped to push forward. A simple thank you seems so inadequate, but know that I am very grateful.

To all my friends and colleagues who shared their gem insights, you have certainly made this book come together! Your stories are so rich in content and I appreciate your willingness to be a part of this awesome experience:

INDIVIDUAL CONTRIBUTORS

Gloria Mayfield Banks – **Detroit, Michigan** - Foreword
Colette Phillips - **Antigua** - Endorsement
Carol Fulp – **New York via St. Thomas** - Endorsement
Guy Churchward – **United Kingdom** – Authenticity
Mithu Bhargava - **India** – Authenticity
Karoline Lariviere - **Germany** - Self-Awareness
R. Siisi Adu-Gyamfi - **Ghana** – Boldness
Dr. Leera Briceno - **Trinidad** - Responsibility
Ivan Espinoza-Madrigal - **Costa Rica** - Responsibility
Betsy Silva - **Puerto Rico** - Faith
Erica Hines - **Jamaica** - Empathy
Patricia Florissi - **Brazil** - Flexibility
Dr. Jean-bernard Charles – **Haiti** - Integrity
Ayman Youssef - **Beirut** – Integrity
Maria DeFatima Barros - **Cape Verde** - Resilience
Subha Barry - **India** – Trust

<u>Gem in Action Participants</u>

Sanian Bailey
Shani Bird
Yogita Inamdar
Trinidad Hermida
Shayla Reed
Catherine Okite
Timothy Davidson

A big thank you to each of you individually and collectively for your time and loving support.

INTRODUCTION

I was raised in a small town on the island of Jamaica. We were poor, yet, my mom created miracles with the very little we had. She did not have a lot of money, but when she cooked she would fill these large oversized pots with her best version of whatever was on the menu for that day. As a child, it appeared as though the entire neighborhood stopped by our house for a meal. In my mind, many of the people were just greedy and wanted to eat all of our food. At times they would come back for a second helping and sometimes even a third. Notwithstanding, no matter how often the same person showed up, I recall Mom saying, "It's just food," and she never got upset or left anyone with an empty plate. We always had more than enough food in the pot. I was too young to realize it at the time, but my mom's sentiments greatly influenced the way I would later come to think about the world and my interactions with the people I encountered. Her response to these individuals and these situations left an indelible mark on my life and thought process.

The year I turned 20, a family in Shawnee Mission, Kansas sponsored me to come to the United States as a nanny. My transition was so difficult that my body reacted violently; my hair started falling out and I experienced rapid weight loss. As an immigrant, I came to this country with nothing. Although my head was spinning from these difficulties, I recognized I had to figure things out quickly and I needed to adjust to my new surroundings, culture and weather. Even dealing with the fact that I was homesick, I knew I had to make a better life for myself and for those who would come after me.

Looking back on that time, I now realize the mailman, the UPS worker and the landscaper were the only people I saw who looked like me. My employers did everything they could to make me feel comfortable and for that I was grateful and I persevered in spite of how I felt. Some memories are particularly hurtful. Once when I took the children for a walk in the neighborhood, occupants of passing cars yelled, "Negro, go home!" I felt humiliated as I was totally unprepared for this kind of hate and evil. On another occasion, when I took the children to the country club, a little girl walked over to me and asked me if I could wash the darkness off my skin because it was dirty. Not only was this shocking, but it hurt me to the core.

Being a nanny for this family was very tedious, and some weeks I would work all seven days and long hours. I did that work for two years to fulfill my green card obligations, after which I relocated to Boston where I had family members. Every now and then, I was reminded of my reality as an immigrant with little to claim. My two to four jobs were meant to remind me that hard work will not kill me but get me closer to the American dream. I was determined to fulfill that dream, and so upon my arrival in Boston, I secured a job as a unit clerk at a prominent hospital working Monday through Friday. On the weekends, I worked at another city hospital.

Relocating to Boston was a huge eye opener and I had to make adjustments to survive the weather. The cold was unbearable. One day as I stood at the bus stop waiting for transportation to my weekend job, the freezing winds whipped through the bus shelter and caused tears to run down my face. I could literally feel the chill in my bones. My toes and fingers were numb and with every inhalation of cold air, the temperature of my body dropped. Old man winter was marking his territory for sure. I watched as cars passed me while I stood in the frigid elements of winter and I imagined how life could be different, in a better way.

Although I understood that the people in the passing cars were strangers, I could not help but think, "When life gets better for me no one will be left at the bus stop." That morning, feeling cold and discouraged, I resolved to help as many people as I could along my path, no matter how small the help might be.

Reflecting on my time at the bus stop some 25 years later, I was now seated in the corporate office of a major technology company, beginning a new assignment as the Vice President and Chief Diversity Officer. I learned so much over the years, met many people and gained amazing experiences in my journey from nanny to executive. I reminisced about my childhood years in Jamaica and thought about my mom. I couldn't help but wonder what she would think if she could see me now. Feeling certain that she would be proud of my many accomplishments and successes. I was now facing the end of one chapter in my professional life and the start of a new chapter. Even though I was excited and full of anticipation about the unknown, I must confess that there is something both exhilarating and scary about change.

My email sped across the internet at 9:07 AM.EST. I remember the exact time I sent my resignation letter. The subject line read Gratitude and Thanksgiving. Cyberspace carried the correspondence to a wide audience of internal and external colleagues. A few moments later, responses to the news began to flood my inbox. There must have been five hundred or more emails in total. As I read through several of the responses a common theme emerged. It was a thread of gratitude from those whom I had "Lifted as I Climbed." This was noted and expressed in multiple email messages and phone conversations. Below are some of the comments I received:

"You have lifted so many people, and you have changed the lives of so many."

"Everything I learned, I learned from you."

"You lift people up."

The compliments were overwhelming yet humbling. In that moment, I realized I had made a greater impact on the lives of others than I would have ever thought. The emails and phone calls recounted how my mentoring efforts had resulted in promotions, new career paths, and attainment of personal goals. The more gratitude and congratulations I read, the more I recognized that I had made good on that secret promise I made to myself some twenty five years ago while standing at the bus stop on that blistering cold winter morning. Indeed, I had not passed anyone by—not on my watch. The universe has a way of giving back to us as we give.

There are many reasons people do not help or give back to others. Some feel that if they help someone they will be diminished by that person becoming more successful than them. Others believe individuals receiving the help are ungrateful and will soon forget their kindness once they have achieved their goals. This book offers tips, tools and a roadmap describing how to lift someone as you climb without feeling insecure, put upon, or in fear of being taken for granted.

It is in the spirit of continuing to give that I wrote this book. My life is a testament to the power of belief, persistence, commitment, resilience, integrity and goodwill. *Lift As I Climb* is my small contribution to those of you who may doubt that you have what it takes to realize those supersized dreams you have for your career, your family and your life. This book is a collection of gems I learned and lived by as an immigrant girl working my way to the top ranks in corporate America. Each gem is presented as a power word in a dedicated chapter. Each chapter explains and describes how to use the gem in different areas of your life. Within each chapter, I provide concrete examples and share personal stories describing how these gems facilitated my career climb. The gems are enhanced by descriptions of how other immigrants employed them in their own lives. I am confident that our stories will inspire you to blaze trails and make a difference.

As you read these pages, it is my hope that you become even bolder in your endeavors. I challenge you to be more resilient, to persevere in the face of adversity, and to never give up in your journey to attain all you dream to acquire. Embrace who you are, no matter where you hail from or your humble beginnings. Don't ever forget that there is greatness in uniqueness.

When you are finish reading this book you should be motivated to:

- Identify which gems you need to focus on in your personal and professional life
- Conduct an inventory checklist of those you have lifted and those you are continuing to lift. If your list is short you will want to start adding a few more individuals.
- Acknowledge how easy and rewarding it is to lift as you climb.
- Learn more about the life journey of an immigrant. Keep in mind that we are all immigrants unless were born Native Americans. The book will help you no matter where you fall on the immigrant spectrum, whether you are a third or fourth generation immigrant.
- Help existing and new immigrants to reach for the stars and never give up.

GEM ONE

AUTHENTICITY

"The authentic self is the soul made visible."

Sarah Ban Breathnach ~ Author

When I arrived in this country, I was ashamed of my accent. Don't ask me why, but somehow I felt that my accent led people to believe I was less competent, less deserving, and less driven. For years I beat myself up about something I could not readily change about who I am. It was evident that I was not comfortable in my own skin, or at least I thought that everyone knew I wasn't. There were many opportunities I shied away from during my climb in corporate America because of my distinct West Indian accent. Even while I was in several high-level positions, I dodged speaking in large groups, fearing they would judge me based on my accent, rather than my skills, expertise, and talents. I would literally exhaust myself trying to think of ways to avoid center stage.

The day I finally confronted my self-imposed shame of speaking with an accent will always stand out for me. Confronting my shame with the encouragement of a wonderful friend, became a game changer for me. My best friend Gloria Mayfield Banks and I were in a hotel room practicing a speech I was preparing to give in a few days. Obviously, she could tell I was nervous not only about the speech itself, but also about enunciating with complete clarity—in a manner that would be expected from an American born citizen. I was having trouble pronouncing the letters "S," "E," and "D." My pronunciation of these letters was way off the mark – and you could just forget about hearing me try an "H." In the midst of my frustration and discomfort, Gloria interjected a simple yet profound suggestion. "Jackie," she said, "why don't you just own your accent?" Hmm. I thought to myself that sounds like a radical but practical idea. Needless to say, Gloria suggested I slow down and not rush through my talk. Her words were some of the best advice anyone could have given me at that moment. That day in the hotel room was life changing for me. From then on, I owned my accent, who I was, and who I was becoming. One seemingly small gesture made all the difference for me. Instead of hiding, I could shine. So, let me take a moment to formally introduce myself to you. "Hello, my name is Jackie Glenn and I hail from the sunny island of Jamaica." This introductory statement became my signature opening for most, if not all of my speaking engagements.

Rather than seeing myself as someone who tries to fit in and be like everyone else around me, I owned my accent and proudly accepted it as a differentiator. How freeing that acceptance was for me! Today, around the world, no matter where I go to speak and give presentations, I am known as "the woman with the accent." It has become such a selling point for me and a brand that is undeniably authentic. There have been many times when I exited a stage and was greeted by immigrants who expressed pride in themselves simply because they were in the presence of someone who courageously accepted herself, along with her island accent and everything that came with being an immigrant girl. I have heard so many stories of people who felt the same way I did upon arriving in America. They were bashful because of their accent and even shunned advancements or were denied opportunities because of their immigration status. I choose to believe there is awesomeness in diversity, because there is much more to savor in a pot filled with variety and seasoned with flavor. What makes you different can literally propel your career or push you toward your objectives, while opening up greater possibilities for you. More importantly, it can become your brand.

My accent, once a source of shame, was now a catalyst to connect with my audience and capture my distinct brand. On many occasions, people would say to me, "You made me feel so proud to be an immigrant because you just owned it." That alone is incredibly freeing and liberating. Owning every part of me gave me permission to own my gifts, talents and any possibility for advancement that would come my way. There is identifiable confidence in the realness of who you are and that should not be taken for granted. All the quirks about you must be accepted, appreciated, and valued for what they are. They are contributors to your unique identity. Until you can love all of who you are, you will lack the confidence to be all you were designed to be, do and have. When you are grounded in loving yourself, everything about you results in self-assuredness. Self-assuredness breeds a sense of contentment, not the type of contentment that is lazy or unpresuming, but a spirit of peace and ease. At times when the feelings of doubt arise, I intentionally remember to call myself out. One time I had to introduce a prominent celebrity to an audience and I was asked to read directly from the script I had been given prior to going up on stage. Everything was going well until I came across a word that I could not pronounce I finally just spelled it and then I said to the audience, "Okay guys, I think we all know the word." To my surprise, the audience clapped and laughed.

They were accepting of my inabilities and flaws because I was comfortable and I owned it. The celebrity got a kick out of my stumble and when she came on stage to join me, she said "Jackie, I don't even know how to say the word myself." The power of authenticity is amazing, and we both realized the magnitude of this reality. The confidence of knowing who you are frees you to "be" regardless of the situation or circumstance. This allows you to celebrate who you are and embrace others for who they are as well. I have seen people lose their way and vacillate in their ideas and beliefs because they lacked self-assuredness and contentment in who they were. I encourage you to be authentic about who you are, with all of your abilities and inabilities. Know that there is a special place carved out that only you can fill. Bring your authentic self everywhere you go.

<u>Gem Takeaways:</u>

- Be comfortable with yourself.
- Embrace all your "so called" flaws.
- It is always easier to be yourself, knowing that no one can be you like you can.
- You will find people who will identify with you.
- Your uniqueness will be a brand differentiator.

GUY CHURCHWARD
UNITED KINGDOM

Chief Executive Officer

———————◆———

I am originally from England, I didn't live anywhere for a substantial period as my family moved around quite a bit. My last port of call was Cambridge in England before I moved to the United States of America in 1996 to sunny Santa Cruz, California. I am a techie by trade, but most people see me as a business savvy technical executive I suppose. I had travelled every road many times in the U.K. and really fancied a change. I always loved America so when my boss in the Bay Area basically offered me a position. I took it.

Authenticity is very important to me and I'm sure people use the term differently. For me, however, it conjures up terms like honesty, real, and transparency. My dad instilled a few moralistic codes in me, one of which was when you are working for a company, be who you are and if they do not like it then go where they do. I have always lived by that sentiment and that is why the idea of authenticity is so fundamental to my personal brand.

The Fortune 500 IT Company where I worked was growing fast, requiring me to interview a lot of people. As I interviewed various candidates, I began noticing a common thread. These were internal and external candidates and they would basically say, "I do not know what it is. I am not sure how to put my finger on it, but there is a buzz around your organization and everybody I talked to is so authentic." I began to understand that this was a key attribute of our group, something fundamental that created excitement and success. I am very transparent and candid and so you get the good side and the bad side. I think that if you can be the best of who you are and who you aspire to be and if you feel comfortable to be yourself in the job, then you will contribute, blossom and thrive. That's how I describe authenticity, being able to express your true self. Life's too short for tap dancing. People respect honesty and candor but many fear showing weakness so they hide behind bravado and fast words.

If you can admit to yourself what you are good at and specifically if you can comfortably admit to people what you are bad at, then two things happen:

1. You understand more about who you are and how to excel.
2. You realize what you are not very good at and what you don't like doing, then hopefully

somebody will pick that bit up and run with it because they want to help you be successful.

I believe people struggle with being authentic because they fear being called out. In essence, everyone is generally good at some things, average at others and kind of crappy at the rest. Tell people the truth because if you profess that you are good at everything then the worst thing might happen, and you end up being measured exclusively on something you were hoping didn't matter and you are not equipped to handle.

If you can literally see yourself in the mirror for who you are, you can understand what brand you have, accept what you are not good at and admit to people what you are good at. It is then you can find peace and value in your lot and build a successful and fulfilling life.

You can be authentic because you have nothing to hide. Authenticity is a lot deeper than the word, it's a code of ethics to live by. The goal is simply to be the very best version of yourself or help someone be the very best version of themselves, and that takes bravery.

MITHU BHARGAVA
INDIA

Senior Vice President &
General Manager

———————◆———————

I am a first-generation immigrant woman who came to the United States of America almost two decades ago with the goal of pursuing a higher education, and the dream of a better future

As I reflect on my journey and who I am today - I am taken back to my early, formative years as a young girl growing up in India. I was fortunate enough to be nurtured by a set of parents who raised me to believe that I was more than equal to anyone else out there, and that there was nothing I couldn't achieve if I set my mind to it. I believe this innate confidence that I developed early on, has hugely influenced my way of thinking and my approach to life in general. Through the years, while I may have been perceived as being different or considered "less equal" as a young girl, a woman, or an immigrant, in my mind I was completely blind to this perception. I held onto the philosophy that I could achieve anything I set my mind to, and over time this became my life mantra. This has served me well in overcoming the many challenges one encounters in life, be it at a professional level as I built my career to reach senior leadership positions in a largely male dominated environment, or at a personal level, balancing continued education, motherhood, family and life all together!

While confidence came naturally to me, learning to be "authentic" was a journey. When I think about authenticity, it's bigger than just *being yourself*. It

7

is about - *embracing yourself, the complete you*. Honestly, even for someone like myself who is seemingly confident, it took me several years to truly understand and embrace every aspect of me – the woman in me, the immigrant in me, every aspect of me that was different and unconventional. It was an evolution to get to the point where I felt that authenticity was embodied in my leadership signature, and it was truly reflective of the complete me.

To elaborate on my journey to true authenticity – I was fortunate to have been considered for many opportunities that helped me accelerate my career, but required me to be tough, unemotional and aggressive. The behaviors I saw around me modelled much of the same, and were arguably table stakes for the job. Over time, these traits were clearly reflected in the image I portrayed. I was no different than the rest, and I fit in perfectly with everyone else around me. However, with time and experience, I realized that the person I came across as was only *a part of me*. I started to evolve my thinking to include my values and my culture into the image I portrayed. Interestingly, I learned that it was okay to be different, in fact it was an advantage.

Eventually I transformed my approach to blend both professional and personal traits that were important to me into the person I portrayed I was, be it at, or outside of work. For example - I allowed people to see the compassionate side of me, that I had so carefully guarded this far. In turn, this balanced their perception of who I was and gave them a better understanding of the bold actions I might need to take on the job. Once I let my guard down and presented who I was, both the good and the bad, I saw people embrace me, and I became more successful at building meaningful relationships with the people around me.

When I think about authenticity today, and how it's embedded in the way people perceive me, I am at the first step of really perceiving myself to be different and really, really embracing it. I do not try to confine to a norm or hold back any part of me. I think it is easier to simply be yourself. There are those that may not necessarily appreciate your authenticity, but you still have to be yourself. You can use your uniqueness to your advantage.

Over the years, I've often been told "you come off as very authentic." Each time I hear that, I can't help but laugh out loud. It has been a very long and interesting journey to get here.

GEM TWO

SELF-AWARENESS

"Self-awareness gives you the capacity to learn from your
mistakes as well as your successes. It enables you to keep growing."

Lawrence Bossidy ~ Retired CEO, AlliedSignal

Self-awareness is being aware of your "whole self," with all of your characteristics and quirks.

These will all contribute to the holistic 'you' and allow you to come to the table grounded and secure in who you are as a person. However, now is also probably a good time to stop and consider how we present our self-awareness. We are sometimes so firm in our identity and experiences that we can be somewhat belligerent about our beliefs. It is easy to think that others should know and accept our views.

So, as you look within, conduct a quick self-assessment. In each of your actions and interactions, ask yourself: Is it kind? Is it necessary? Is it true? If your answer to all three questions is "yes," then you can proceed with confidence. However, if your response to any of the three questions is no, then you should take some time for additional consideration. Am I being close minded, inflexible and rigid in my beliefs? What is my motive? Go through your checks and balances to make sure you never lose sight of your reasons for doing or saying what you do.

In a conversation I once stated, "You know I've been on the international stage for many years, showing up and repeating my standard introduction, "My name is Jackie Glenn. I am the Chief Diversity Officer / Vice President." I have traveled the world extensively throughout my career. The second phase of becoming more self-aware moves me to ask these questions…is recognition and being onstage what I'm living for? Is that my identity? Or is my identity the values and morals I hold dear? If I am out of the spotlight, will I still be Jackie? How am I waking up today? Am I being intentional, deliberate, and purposeful? I think once you start to think on this level, your introspection leads to the following question: what am I doing to be of service to someone else? That someone could be a loved one or anyone we come in contact with on a daily basis. This is where the lift model starts to come alive and take shape, because you are now willing to be of service not only to yourself, but also to those around you. This phase of self-awareness moves you to be of service and help someone else achieve their goals by employing the strategies you used to achieve yours.

I travel a great deal and being self-aware allows me to confidently practice the familiar guidance, "when in Rome, do as the Romans do." So, when I go anywhere, I really try to take on the culture and practices of the region. As a diversity expert when I am in India, I wear my Sari. A couple of fat rolls might be exposed, but that's irrelevant. When I spoke on St Patrick's Day in Ireland, I strutted on that stage in my green St. Patrick leather skirt with a pink top and they loved it. Talk about a reception! The audience's response was loud and approving, all because I joined in their celebration of St. Patrick's Day. I was there with them and I really believe that if you meet people in their space, they will be even more receptive to you. I'm not going to shave my head if I go to a place where everybody is shaving their head. However, in my travels I've learned that when people see that you are making an effort to know and understand their culture, they become much more accepting of you. It frees you up to be who you are, and shows that you are open to celebrate others. From there, the possibilities are endless.

Learning to lighten up a bit and not be so hard on yourself is a sign that you're becoming self-aware and more comfortable in your own skin.

The word I use is contentment. No one is perfect, and so I encourage myself to do my best. Even people who speak the King's English make mistakes sometimes. In the end, it's about giving yourself permission and the latitude to be yourself and to just show up. So, when I'm asked to define self-awareness in my lift model, I reply that self-awareness, in its simplest term is being aware of yourself, who you are and what are some of your traits and quirks.

Knowing your strengths, your areas for improvement, and your faults are all part of being self-aware. It is being cognizant of how you appear and how you are perceived. Even if some of that perception is not favorable, you know what it is you need to work on. In the absence of self–awareness in your life, this can lead to career derailment and a downward spiral. There was a time when the feedback and evaluations I received stated, "Jackie presents herself very confidently in everything she does. She's straightforward, tough, no nonsense, and sometimes she can come across as very aggressive to the point where people are afraid of her." Some of my managers have even gone as far as saying, "You know Jackie, you show up so strong that even though you might be saying the right things, the way you come across is so demanding and so forceful that people don't even want to talk to you." While I did not like that those were the words used to describe me, I have heard it so many times that I am very much aware of how I am perceived. So I began to own it! I owned it in knowing that I needed to change, become more introspective and do somethings differently. Not that I am a chameleon, but I understand that when I am showing up in certain places, some individuals can accept that I come across strong and others cannot. So, if I don't know the audience I am standing before, I go in being a lot more self-aware and recognize that in certain settings there are things that I should and should not say. In some cases, I count to ten when I am going to respond to something that's controversial, that boils my blood, and makes me really want to jump up out of my seat and go for the jugular. This is my self- awareness at work.

I often practice thinking to myself and saying, "Okay, Jackie, be aware of how that's going to come across," and I check myself and come out a little less overly excited. Sometimes people take my excitement and my passion on particular subjects as aggression and being a bully; when in fact, I'm just passionate about my point of view and my intent is not to be mean spirited. I find that in instances like those, I do a lot of self-editing and self-regulating to make sure my tone is conducive to a dialogue instead of a show down or a fight.

Another example of how I have changed my approach is captured in this following anecdote: I walked into a conference room and I sat down in front of my supervisor. She said, "Jackie, you know..." and she started telling me all of the great things I had done. "But," she said, "I just have to tell you that people are really afraid of you." I became emotional but I quickly calmed myself down and asked, "Can you explain to me how I appear? What does that look like? Give me an example of when people are afraid of me. What am I doing that makes people afraid of me?" She replied, "You raise your voice, you talk over people and you shut people down." I persisted, and I asked my supervisor to give me a more detailed example of perhaps an instance when such behavior was on display, because I welcome this feedback and I'm even more intent on working to improve. I evaluated her feedback and took what I need to work on and remained true to my core values.

One of the things I have learned over time and continue to apply the more experienced I become is, never being afraid to say I am wrong or I am sorry. This has become an easy phrase for me. With time I have learned a few invaluable lessons. First, constantly ask for feedback, especially when you have a forceful personality like mine. A lot of people would be afraid to give you feedback if you are that direct, but keep asking nonetheless. This will aid you in receiving a true gauge of how you are being perceived, because sometimes people will not be honest in their critique of your style. Getting different perspectives helps to give an accurate picture of how you show up. You are looking for constructive feedback, so keep asking different individuals as you go, and be sure to also ask how you could have handled the situation better.

An equally valuable lesson is to "turn the table", putting myself in the other person's shoes. I have learned to ask, would I appreciate being treated that way? Don't be afraid to peel back the onion, look inwardly and do some self-examination. It's an opportunity for me to immediately take stock of myself and see what I could have done better. I continue to learn and consider myself a lifelong learner. Here is a story, we were at a staff meeting and I was the only black person there and one of three women. One of the male on the team started a discussion about not having enough diversity in the sales force. He told us about a saleswoman who was contemplating legal action against the company and further stated that this is why we don't want to hire minorities and women because they are litigious. Now this was a colleague making that statement, I interrupted him and I said, "Shame on you. You are supposed to be advocating for these individuals, especially in your role and this is what's coming out of your mouth? "

Everyone was stunned that I was so direct in my feedback regarding his comment. His response was "maybe it didn't come out the right way." After the meeting my manager called me into the office and he said, "Jackie, you were right, but it's the way you did it, not allowing him to finish making his point you just shut him down." Some of my colleagues approached me and expressed their thanks for speaking up because they were so stunned and caught off guard they could not respond. There are times when we need to address situations immediately. So, regardless of how my manager felt about my handling of the situation, this was not a subconscious move on my part. I was deliberate in letting this colleague know that his behavior was unacceptable and would not be tolerated. Whenever you need additional help with evaluating your actions or reactions, I encourage you to create a personal Board of Directors. This familiar concept means having a select group of people whom you trust to give you direct feedback in a variety of situations. Your personal board members should be people who will be there to assist you but also hold you accountable for your actions.

Gem Takeaways:

- Be open to feedback and although it is easier said than done, stay open to everything.
- Do a self- awareness assessment at least every other year.
- Develop a personal Board of Directors.
- Some of the best feedback I received was from people I perceived did not like me.
- Be a lifelong learner.
- Saying I am sorry or please forgive me does not make you weak.

KAROLINE LARIVIERE
GERMANY

Senior Vice President,
Human Resources

It would be nice to think that knowing how to do something really well or delivering perfect results will make us great leaders. Unfortunately, that's just not true.

I grew up in Hamburg Germany, which has the charm of a port city like Boston and the cultural diversity and energy of a metropolitan city like Manhattan. An only child of two strict German parents, I learned early that I had to be prepared, I had to have a strong defensible position when I was asking for things (because "Debbie's parents let her" was just not compelling enough!) —and I had to be able to back it up with facts. In other words, I had to make sure I got it right.

When I started working, taking the same approach that served me so well with my parents, in school and in college, seemed like a logical choice. Oh boy, did I get that wrong. You have to know what you're doing at work, that's the starting point. Having said that, people don't like working with a know-it-all and employees don't like to be managed by someone who always thinks they're right. When I was starting out, it didn't occur to me that knowing something really well wouldn't be enough. Thankfully I figured out early enough in my career that it's more important to be effective than it is to be right.

What does this mean and what does that looks like 'out there'? It doesn't mean that you're wrong - it means that you don't have to prove you're right. It means hearing people out, it means considering other perspectives and other ideas. It means influencing an outcome versus directing an outcome. We see it all the time that newly minted VP or CEO who believes their promotion made them smarter than everyone else. They seem like they have something to prove and proceed to "tell" everyone what to do and micromanage everything within an inch of its life. In their minds they are the experts, and no one can do it as well as them. What they are doing is managing teams, but they certainly aren't leading them. In order to be a leader, you need people to follow – not because of your title, but because you inspire them, and they feel valued.

In my work as an HR partner and coach to executives, I come across this, too. Over the years, I've also come to realize that part of this often has to do with a fear of failure. Let's go back to that newly minted CEO who comes out of the gate a little too hot. They are probably afraid of failure and think proving they are right will make them successful. They come on too strong, step on people, and in some cases go so far that it's not recoverable. In those situations, they often come to me and say, "But that's not what I meant when I did that". Of course, those were not their intentions. Self-awareness can be hard to come by but can bring you a long way. Did they read the room when they were presenting? Did they catch people making eye contact with each other but not them, did they pick up on the change in tone, or the way no one asked any questions or offered any ideas? Probably not. And a softer position based on common goals is much more effective in influencing an outcome, than taking a strong position with only your own goal in mind.

What do I say to executives when they are meeting with their new teams, when they are trying to get the CEO or the Board to approve something, or when they are trying to negotiate a deal? I ask them: In this moment, is it more important for you to be right *(prove to them how smart you are and probably not win)* or to be effective *(and win, but maybe not in the exact way you want)*? It opens a whole new way of thinking about and approaching situations. And by the way, it works in any relationship interaction!

GEM THREE

BOLDNESS

———————◆◄———————

*"Unless you choose to do great things with it,
it makes no difference how much you are rewarded,
or how much power you have."*

Oprah Winfrey ~ Philanthropist, American Media Proprietor

When one thinks of boldness, the word confidence immediately comes to mind. If both qualities are practiced correctly you can achieve great things. My definition of boldness/confidence is being sure of what you know while knowing who you are. The mindset of believing that you can achieve anything you put your mind to is a must. People who choose to be bold are inspiring not just because they get big things accomplished, but also because they instigate growth, progress, and movement for themselves and others around them. Sadly, far too many people wait for someone who is bold to lead the way, hoping somehow luck will bring success. Boldness is our willingness to venture out and do the right thing at the right time, regardless of the barriers or fears we may encounter. This enables us to speak the truth and perform a task without fear of the consequences or results, because it is the right thing to do.

Boldness should never be mistaken for being rude and abrasive; you always want to practice being bold but never rude. A bold spirit is kind, patient and collaborative. It allows others to express themselves and their opinions. This gem is important in every area of our lives personally, professionally and also in our faith. A lack of boldness can be problematic as it will stifle or derail one's career or life goals. It will also hold you back from progress, affect relationships and prevent you from becoming all that you can be. At times you have to exercise your boldness muscle even if it means being vulnerable and results in criticism. Cowardice, fearfulness, cynicism, negativity, discouragement, and pessimism are all opposites of boldness. These traits create a negative attitude that is infectious to others and should be intentionally called out and avoided.

I must confess that it is not natural for me to always practice this gem; one way that I do so is by adding a bit of humor which lightens the situation and gives me a chance to get my point across. Whenever I employ this approach I am almost always asked to say more, and that is when I use this gem to make my position clear. When I first became Chief Diversity Officer, I had an opportunity to present to the CEO and his direct reports. When my manager and I entered the boardroom, all the seats around the table were occupied and the occupants were all Caucasian males. My manager and I were both super nervous. We were the only women in the room. The only seats available to us were in the back or on the side as none of the men made an attempt to include us around the table.

Immediately my boldness and authenticity kicked in along with a bit of humor. I grabbed a chair and did something I would never think of doing for fear of how I would be perceived. I went right next to the CEO and said one of my favorite Jamaican expressions, "Small up yourself," which meant make room for my chair. At that moment, everyone busted out laughing and the CEO moved around the table to make room for my chair. In a very short period of time everyone followed the leader and I repositioned my chair next to the CEO. Internally, I applauded myself for being bold. I honestly could not foresee the outcome but I took the chance and was prepared for the consequences.

My manager was uncomfortable, so she went and sat at the back of the room. As the only black woman in the boardroom, I was determined to be around the table. After all, they had invited us to the table. So where was the seat? The fact that they did not make an effort to reposition themselves when we walked into the room made me realize that it was my job to be bold and confident. My intention was not to be abrasive. I did not have an attitude nor was I trying to be controversial. I just thought that it was the right thing to do at the right time. My act of boldness was a learning experience for everyone in the room. I used my immigrant colloquial expression which created humor and got the desired results - a seat at the table. This moment of humor also helped to break the tension in the boardroom. Now everyone was relaxed enough to hear what I had to say. They received it well and I was relaxed and able to give my presentation successfully.

Whenever you bring your boldness and self-confidence to the table you gain a sense of satisfaction and accomplishment. When you operate in boldness you can actually produce more and do better for yourself and those around you. The energy created by your boldness evaporates the nervousness you experience when asking, "Am I saying the right thing?" Or, "Am I getting my point across?" Boldness calms you down and brings you poise and grace to do what you are tasked to do. You can actually slow your heart rate down and get your clear and succinct message across. So much more can be realized when we do it with boldness and confidence.

Assume positive intent when you are in the room or in any situation although there may be clear signs that say the opposite. Not everyone wants to hear what you have to say, but there may be a few who do. Focus on them and envision that there are many more of those who want to hear you. Do not allow your internal or self-talk to say: "Oh my gosh, this person is crossing their arms and giving me the side eye, I don't think they want to hear me." Assume that everyone in the room is your friend and move forward with conviction instead of being frozen by your thoughts regarding who is in the room and what they may be thinking or saying about you.

Operating in boldness minimizes the "imposter syndrome," which is also known as impostor phenomenon, fraud syndrome or the impostor experience[1]. These terms describe a psychological pattern in which an individual doubts their accomplishments and has a persistent internalized fear of being exposed as a "fraud." An estimated seventy percent[2] of us likely experience at some point the feelings of inadequacy and "fakeness" that accompanies the Imposter Syndrome.

Success is impossible without the courage to act boldly and it can require taking creative risks, upsetting some people, gambling on your own self-esteem, or in a more literal sense, your self-worth. But you don't find many successful entrepreneurs, politicians, coaches, achievers of any stripe or people with disabilities who will describe themselves as risk-averse. This gem is especially important to people with disabilities or different abilities. Most people with a visible or invisible disability are often reluctant to disclose their status or discuss if it's visible for fear of being subjected to biases or treated differently.

Using the boldness gem will hold people accountable, shine a spotlight on the issue and also make individuals and organizations be more open to looking at the whole person instead of their disability. Unfortunately, sometimes you have to step into your boldness and stand up for yourself and others to get a favorable response. I know it's not easy but having allies who can help is a great way to practice this gem. Only you know how badly you want to get to the next level or to the next dimension and boldness will help you to get there.

Gem Takeaways:

- Boldness and confidence can be learned by practicing in your familiar surroundings.
- Make sure you suspend all judgement and assume positive intent.
- Practice makes perfect.
- Add a bit of humor.
- Remember exhibiting boldness and confidence requires bravery.

R. SIISI ADU - GYAMFI
GHANA

Managing Partner, AGA & CEO

My dreams of coming to America began for me when I was in third grade and realized President Kennedy initiated the USAID program in my country, Ghana. I began preparing myself for the opportunity to go to school in America. Eventually, my dreams became reality when I was admitted to the Massachusetts Institute of Technology (MIT). Freshman year at MIT taught me many things, among them was that I needed to challenge myself to be successful. My first grading period was a disaster. While school had been easy for me in Ghana, I needed to change my approach for success at MIT. My efforts were rewarded when at graduation, my name was called three times to receive three degrees.

Employment in America brought different challenges. However, the two proverbs by which I live fueled my success. They are: "Be not afraid of growing slowly, be afraid of standing still" (Chinese Proverb) and "A changed place cannot transform an individual but a transformed individual can change a place" (African Proverb). Additionally, I brought that spirit of relishing a challenge to my work. I was willing to take confident risks (be bold) in my work to make a difference.

One such example occurred in the 1980s when the company I worked for wanted another company to port their software to the company's platform. Several executives from my company had gone to Brussels to convince the company's CEO to port. However, each visit yielded nothing. The reason given was that the CEO was not interested in porting. I asked my boss to give a colleague and I a final shot to meet with the CEO. I was way down the corporate ladder, but my boss thought it would not hurt. My colleague and I made the trip to Belgium and met with the CEO.

"Welcome. You have 30 minutes," the CEO said.

"Our goal today is a simple one. We came to listen to your needs," I said.

"You don't have a presentation to give?" the CEO asked.

"No, we don't. We came to listen," I replied.

This surprised the CEO. He had become imbued with presentations from our company that touted how great we were and paid little attention to his needs. The CEO went on to explain his issues and after a two-hour meeting, he agreed to port the software, subject to a couple of conditions. This breakthrough meeting happened because I boldly volunteered to have a crack at the CEO.

From my experience, there are a few traits and proverbs important to expressing boldness:

- Core Values. You must have strong core values. "The ruins of a nation begin in the homes of its people." -- Ashanti proverb
- Competence. You must be competent and know your stuff. "Lack of knowledge is darker than night." --African proverb
- Communication. Effective communication is non-negotiable. "A pearl is worthless as long as it is in its shell." -- Indian proverb
- Credibility. Without credibility it is difficult to motivate others to listen to you or to follow you. "One falsehood spoils a thousand truths." – Ashanti proverb
- Champions. Mentors are important in this role so look for mentors at different levels in your personal and professional development.......black, white, brown, male, female all can make a huge difference in your life.

- "He who treats you as himself does no injustice." – Lon proverb
- Community. Give Back. Mentor and encourage others. "We are linked in both life and death. Those who share common relations never break apart." – Ashanti proverb
- Charisma. You need that air about you. Be charming, be a magnet to draw people to you.
- "The eyes that have seen an ocean cannot be satisfied by a mere lagoon." – African proverb

GEM FOUR

RESPONSIBILITY

"Leaders inspire accountability through their ability to accept responsibility before they place blame."

Courtney Lynch ~ Author

Hard work is a subject that I am very passionate about, and when I think of hard work, I always think of responsibility and accountability. I truly believe that my passion stems from my immigrant upbringing. Personally, I am programed to believe that I am accountable to anyone who gives me the opportunity to do a job and attaches a reward to it whether it is monetary or in kind. My sense of responsibility encourages me to do my best, and to go above and beyond expectations. I believe in putting my best foot forward with an outcome that is "shining with excellence" because accountability is the only way for me with or without being compensated.

One has to develop the fundamental traits of accountability and responsibility in order to be successful. These traits are also necessary to get to the next level in achieving your desired goals. Remember that your name and brand are on the line when you take on a job. Hiring you is a sign that your employer has put their trust in you and they are confident that you will work hard and will truly earn your wages. They are sure your effort will be worth the investment. Revisiting my work before I do a hand over or completeness check is a consistent process. If after careful scrutiny, my work does not reflect my personal brand, I have no problem with a complete do-over. Hard work really is about taking responsibility and owning what you committed to do. It is also taking responsibility to ensure that work is completed with excellence.

Each of us has a brand whether we are aware of it or not. This is what you would want individuals to say about you when you are not in the room. Companies, charities, schools, professional individuals etc. work hard and spend top dollar to perfect their brand so that they can stand above their competitors. If you want your brand to be like the Ritz Carlton, you must work on achieving that standard. I work very hard and take every opportunity to ensure that my brand reflects what I truly believe. When the name Jackie Glenn comes up, I want my branding to stand for hard working, someone who does what she says she's going to do, and someone with a reputation for excellence. This does not come easy, and one must be willing to put in the hard work even if it means doing the same task over and over again to get it right.

Excellence should be the goal, as anything less than clouds your brand. For example, my career path afforded me the opportunity to manage a team globally as a Chief Diversity Officer. At one point, I was getting feedback from my manager that people were nervous around me. She let me know that I was going to have to figure something out because she was getting complaints from individuals that they were intimidated to the point they thought they were being bullied. Needless to say this feedback was crushing.

Even though my feelings were hurt by these statements, I decided to take action, take full responsibility and become accountable for how I was being perceived. This was my brand which was now being affected. One of the things I decided to do was to get a personal coach to help me redefine the way I show up. Although I knew I was not intentionally trying to be mean, rude, harsh or frightening to anyone. Accepting the hard fact that I was coming across that way to others I went back to the old analogy that I used earlier on, took responsibility and accepted the feedback.

My manager once told me, "Jackie, I know that if you have something to do you will stay here all night until you get it done. You will work your tail off to produce good work even if it means bringing a cot into the office to sleep on. You will do whatever it takes to meet your deadline." These words were hugely affirming for me because she recognized and knew of my past performance, that I would get the job done well. She also stated that I needed to realize not everyone has the same work ethic, recognizes the challenge I face when dealing with employees that were irresponsible and that I believed employees should work for their wages. I could not disagree with this observation because it was the truth. However, my holding people accountable and responsible made some extremely uncomfortable.

Eventually, I learned the importance of letting employees know my expectations at the beginning of our working relationship. I now establish and provide directions, expectations and standards at the start of their employment. This crucial piece, up front, can avoid a great deal of stress, offense and misunderstanding later. When setting these early expectations, I let my team members know they will be held responsible and accountable for the job they were hired to do, they will need to work to match my effort, and if they are having a challenge matching my efforts we need to communicate and have a dialogue about how we can move forward. This included a very important accountability piece that allows the employee an opportunity to respond to the following concerns:

- Will you let me know if I have offended you?
- Have I asked you to do something you really cannot get to within the required time frame?
- How would you like to receive feedback?

When you set those expectations around responsibility and accountability you will attract great people on your team, both personally and professionally. I have seen accountability in action on many occasions. Once when I had a critical deadline, one of my team members told me "I can't stay late with you because I have to go home but know that once I put the kids to bed, I will hop back online and finish things up." This is where I feel accountability comes into play, prioritizing and still getting the job done. Responsibility and accountability can really work nicely when everyone on the team is working together to meet achievable goals. I believe everything gets better when dialogue is possible and we are open and transparent.

With clear expectations, individuals achieve more and everyone can be on the same page. Responsibility and accountability work not just on the job but in every area of your life. Excuses and partial acceptance of accountability does not relieve you of your responsibility. For this gem to work effectively, communication is key. For example, if an employee is responsible to be somewhere at a certain time and does not show up and does not provide the manager with an update, this employee is exhibiting a failure to communicate. When you go silent, you are being irresponsible and you're not being accountable for your side of the deal. I think communicating is a core pillar of being responsible.

Most people sets the expectation that they're going to be a hard worker. I don't think anyone gets up in the morning and says, I'm going to be a slumper-dinker and I'm never going to work hard. I am conscious of the fact that everyone's view of hard work is different, but even with this difference, responsibility and hard work still play a key function to success. Individuals should set the hard work expectations base on what they are tasked to do.

I observe young college/university students who struggle with the transition to professional work life. This is seen in their lack of punctuality, getting to work on time, completing a task with efficiency, or volunteering to take on a challenging assignment. If I had to a select a gem that is critical to the success of college and university students, I would choose this gem, responsibility and accountability. As a leader who has coached and mentored dozens of talented young graduates, I believe that responsibility and accountability are competencies they must master.

Gem Takeaways:

- Take responsibility for your actions whether you are right or wrong.
- Successful people always hold themselves accountable, especially when they are leaders.
- Accountability and responsibility are key attributes that employers look for in candidates.
- Accountability and responsibility are key focus areas for college and university students.

DR. LEERA BRICENO
TRINIDAD & TOBAGO

Dermatologist

———————————◆————————

As president and one of the founding partners of South Shore Dermatology Physicians, a six-physician dermatology group in North Easton, Massachusetts, I am expected to a life of responsibility and accountability privately and professionally. I am an immigrant from the Caribbean islands of Trinidad and Tobago who migrated to the United States in 1978 at the age of seventeen along with my mother and siblings.

I am honored to discuss the gem of responsibility in the context of my own life. Responsibility has been one of the guiding principles on which I was raised. It was such a significant part of the foundation of my upbringing in every aspect of my early life I feel 'responsibility' is encoded in my DNA. My father's mantra was that his children were always expected to be respectful. Our main responsibility was to bring our best selves to school every day, to perform at our utmost best and to strive to earn the highest grades possible.

The word *responsibility* is derived from the root word respond, which calls on us to own and to respond appropriately to the issue at hand and to manage that issue successfully. To that end, I can think of a no more consequential field than healthcare where responsibility can have profound consequences if not taken seriously.

As physicians, we take an oath to honor the responsibility of managing and preserving the health of our fellow man. In my own medical training and as I mentor young physicians, the importance of truly owning that responsibility has never been clearer. I have learned and I teach to those who will care for the patients of tomorrow, that deciding to shirk that responsibility can truly lead to significant morbidity and in the worst of circumstances to mortality of those we vow to care for. Other virtues, that go along with responsibility include, an attitude of caring, empathy, dedication, accountability and a commitment to the work. If it is your goal to have success in any aspect of your life, acknowledgement and acceptance of the responsibilities that come in that role are critical ingredients in the recipe for success. In other words, you need to be true to your word to the very end. You need to know that you are in full control of the attitude that you bring to your responsibilities every single day.

Some of the principles that I would share with a mentee in any field, about accountability and responsibility are as follows.

- Step up to claim your portion of the work. Resist fading into the background. Instead, find your role in the grand scheme of things. This attitude of stepping up is one of a leader and shows a willingness to be an integral part of the work.
- Always be good for your word. Execute what you sign up to do and all the while bring your best self and the best of your talents to the table every day.
- Finish what you start. Many people fail because they quit too soon. Seeing the task to the end brings peace of mind in knowing that for better or worse and regardless of the final outcome you have completed what you started. In the role of physician, you would have cared for your patient the way you would want to be cared for every step of the way.

IVÁN ESPINOZA-MADRIGAL
COSTA RICA

Lawyer & Executive Director

———————————◆◆◆———————————

I was born in Costa Rica and I have lived in the United States since I was nine years-old. I was raised by my mother, a single parent.

I am the Executive Director of Lawyers for Civil Rights in Boston, a non-profit legal organization that filed the first lawsuits in the country against the Trump Administration to protect sanctuary cities; to save Temporary Protected Status (TPS) on behalf of Central American immigrants; and to block immigration arrests in courthouses.

In 2018, Lawyers for Civil Rights celebrated its 50th anniversary. We were founded in 1968 at the height of the civil rights movement, and we desegregated the Boston Public Schools and the Boston public housing projects. Fifty years later, we continue advancing life-changing and law-changing civil rights work on behalf of people of color and immigrants.

In the current climate, many people of color and immigrants feel under attack. Life-saving immigration programs are being dismantled at the federal level, and immigration enforcement has become increasingly aggressive. Many people are living in fear. This assault on immigrants is incredibly heartbreaking.

Diversity has always been one of our strengths. We should be learning from – and with – each other across differences. But we have far too many examples of growing social distance between diverse communities. This leads to less empathy across race, zip code, and even political lines. We need to strengthen our capacity to empathize.

Across the country, we need to have more conversations about diversity and inclusion focusing on age, color, creed, disability, gender, gender expression, gender identity, national origin, race, religion, sex, sexual orientation and veteran status. We need to talk about creating meaningful opportunities for empowerment and advancement for everyone. And our motto should be: no one left behind!

We also need to eradicate all forms of hate. At Lawyers for Civil Rights, we provide free legal support to victims of discrimination. Our clients have survived not only deprivations of their constitutional and civil rights, but also traumatic experiences that are designed to rob them of their dignity and humanity. We help our clients assert their rights. We help them to empower themselves, their family, and their community. For example, we recently represented Black twins who were unfairly disciplined for wearing braids to a charter school in Massachusetts. While their classmates altered their hair without consequences, the Black twins' racial and cultural hair expression was met with punishment. We supported the twins as they spoke out, bringing national attention to this problem. Ultimately, the twins scored a major victory and succeeded in changing their school's policy. This incident raises a host of important lessons not only for the classroom, but for the workplace. It is also a powerful reminder that as we interact in our society across differences, we have to respect and embrace all identities and cultures. We should not be in the business of excluding, punishing or penalizing people based on their identity or background.

Finally, it is critically important for everyone in our communities to be able to see themselves reflected in the halls of power from elected offices to corporate board rooms. All of us should be able to see ourselves reflected in our social institutions. And this means that we have to be actively removing systemic barriers and deliberately closing opportunity gaps. We have to be radically inclusive. And we must commit to leaving no one behind!

GEM FIVE

FAITH

---◆---

"The angel went to her and said, "Greetings, you who are highly favored! The Lord is with you.""
St. Luke 1:28(NIV)

Growing up in the island of Jamaica my mom instilled within me her compassionate Christian principles. She taught me the golden rule of doing unto others as I would like them to do unto me, and clearly articulated that trust and belief in God would get me through any and all of life's crises. Over the years I endeavored to practice and develop my faith as I faced challenges in my personal and professional life. Working in Corporate America I learned to draw on my faith like an ever-present electric current, energizing and guiding me. I would always receive wide smiles when I was asked by anyone how I was doing, whether it was the CEO, peers or colleagues. My resounding consistent response would be, "Blessed and highly favored, thank you!" I loved to say this because even though everything was not perfect each time I was asked, my faith reassured me that everything would be alright, and to this day, it still does.

Blessed and highly favored was a constant reminder of my core beliefs. I knew that God had the power to favor and bless me in all of life's peaks and valleys. There were days at work when I had to draw on my faith to get me through some tough circumstances. One day I attended a meeting with the leadership of our sales team, all of whom happened to be white men. The meeting was to discuss diversity metrics, and our presenter was

33

the only other woman in addition to me. At the very onset of presenting the metrics she was met with fierce opposition from the men in the room who stated that the numbers were incorrect. The opposition was so great that she left the room crying before completing the presentation.

As the only other female and a woman of color I sat there astonished at their behavior. After saying a prayer in my heart and asking God for direction, I drew on my inner strength and belief which put me on my feet. Deep inside I felt the fear of being treated the same way or even worse because I was now taking on a distinct and challenging role within this group, with men who outranked me in terms of position and power. Silence swept over the room as everyone anticipated what I was about to say. I asked the question, "Does anyone care to address what just happened here?" No one responded. I then made a comment that you should do unto others as you would have them do unto you. I then told the group I was leaving the room to find the presenter and that when she returned to complete the presentation they should listen and absorb the metrics and not be defensive. There would be plenty of time for respectful dialogue.

This moment of "divine intervention" was definitely my faith at work, because rather than being frozen, I believed that God had given me the power of my own voice and my sound mind. I put my faith into action and remembered that I could do all things through Him who strengthens me. I left the room in search of the presenter because another expression of my faith is always to be present in the form of servant leadership. The character of serving comes naturally for me and our presenter was in need. When I found her she was crying and deeply distraught by the disrespect she had encountered. Once again my faith guided me to tell her that she was not alone and I was there to support her – we were in this together. With newfound strength we went back to the room and she completed the presentation and everyone was respectful and listened to what she had to say. At the end of the meeting the global head of sales called me aside. I was prepared for a reprimand, but instead he commended me for having the courage to speak up and take charge. He concluded by saying he knew there was something different about me. He could not pinpoint what it was but I knew it was my faith at work. I do believe that everyone has a set of faith principles that they summon for guidance, courage, or inspiration. It doesn't matter how your faith shows up; only that it provides a foundation that you can lean on when the need arises. As my career progressed I often had the opportunity to work with individuals from diverse faith backgrounds. Our names for the higher power were different, but when we were in crisis mode everyone drew on their core beliefs and values to get us through; restoring, affirming, and casting a light for us to follow. My core faith and my servant leadership grew in tandem, giving me energy and an outlet that were equally fulfilling.

Today there is a lot of talk by corporate leaders around the idea of servant leadership. My personal definition is that it is a way of leading from the heart, to express our faith at work through intentional actions and care for others. Like all of our behavior, we are at our best when we are absolutely clear on why we do what we do and take full ownership. I have never doubted that one of my greatest joys is helping others. I know that through my loving mother it is in my DNA, resting at the core of my creation. I imagine this deep sense of humanity was formed by my childhood experiences. My mother modeled a spirit of giving and helpfulness at all times and never wavered. Where there was scarcity, she created abundance. We were poor, but we did not know it because of her innovative ways to enrich our lives and strengthen our love. Years later, I would be honored with an award from a leading diversity organization for being a "Trailblazer." I would read a speech highlighting the candid and generous opinions of some wonderful people about the gifts I brought them through my work, my inclusion, my support and my strength. Gifts for the journey, fire for the spirit. What better expression of faith? The ever-present Jamaican girl inside me remembered the trail that led to our kitchen table, and the fire that blazed beneath my mother's pots. My original Trail blazer. This warmth still radiates, now from the inside out.

Throughout my career, my faith has been both a barometer and a lens to balance and guide me. I rarely had anyone to take me under their wings and demonstrate to me how to lead or manage. However, individuals I reported to were always quick to point out when I wasn't doing a task or function correctly, from their standpoint. As a result, mentoring others and leading by coaching became an obsession for me. Inside I knew that I was being a servant leader, helping others by clearing their path and lighting their way (even when the light was a little bright at times!). Most of my career, I felt as if I was being tested by my leaders to see whether I would sink or swim. To their surprise, I always swam. My faith got me through these times. I wasn't always a graceful swimmer, but the reservoir of grace was filled inside me. As a result of my faith I deliberately and intentionally aspired to be an equal opportunity developer by helping anyone who sought me out or worked with me. I wanted to do for others what no one did for me. Blessed and highly favored.

My personal responsibility to my new employees was to teach them as much as I could about my role and the responsibilities of our team. I would encourage them to learn by watching and shadowing others. I invited my employees and those I was mentoring to observe me in action, to get to know my work ethic and to understand that nothing was too small for me to do. Again, servant leadership prompted me to roll up my sleeves and jump in with both feet to help get the job done. I took pride in knowing how to do all the jobs on my team, which gave me valuable insight into their daily opportunities and challenges. The barometer and the lens of faith lets us see if their roles are matched with their talents and passions and calibrate accordingly. When we help bring out the best in others, we provide one of the highest callings of service. This is an essential way that I lift others as I climb. Decades from now, long after I have left this planet, I want my legacy to be the lasting effects of my servant leadership, and hopefully have it passed along to others.

As a servant leader, so many gifts that I have offered have been answered not only with gratitude but with gifts to increase my own knowledge and development. Often when I was expecting to be the mentor, a young voice would say, "Mrs. Glenn, have you ever thought about ..." Or, "Jackie, have you ever considered adding this or doing that?" The resulting dialogue makes life and work so much easier and it lifts me up in the process. Collaborating effectively with multiple generations has been one of the blessings of my life. Always assume someone has a helpful perspective to offer. Your inclusion will almost certainly be rewarded.

Give with a clean and pure heart, without expectation. Your gift may be time, treasure, service, knowledge or a home-cooked meal. When you open yourself, it actually works out better than you expected. Give freely because no one has ever gotten poor from giving.

Gem Takeaways:

- Remember the saying "It's in giving that you receive."
- Being of service doesn't take anything away from who you are; it only builds you up.
- Don't be afraid to bring your faith with you to the workplace as a current that powers you.
- Let your faith step in when doubts arise.
- Serve others without reservation or expectation, the reward will be great.

BETSY SILVA
PUERTO RICO

Global Talent, Inclusion & Leadership Development Executive

Have you ever had this moment of profound reflection regarding your actions in life and you are like…WAIT A MOMENT…WOW…I HAD NEVER REALIZED THIS ABOUT ME… WOW! Writing for this chapter was this WOW moment for me. Let me share with you what transpired.

Jackie called me asking, "Betsy, how does your faith play out in the leadership roles you have held in the corporate world?" It was a profound question. I believe it was the first time I was asked to consider this. Yet as with all that happens in my life, I truly believe that Jackie's call and question were no accident. Why? You see over the past few years, I have found myself curious to understand what it means to have faith. How do I know if I am living in faith? I found that I was examining my actions, hungry to recognize whether I was truly and intentionally living in faith. I feel that the questions I was asking myself about my faith were like a prayer to my heavenly Father. Jackie's call was part of His plan to help me find the answers.

In searching for the answer, I went about it in the only way I knew how, which was to watch the tape titled Betsy's Life's Journey. It was like watching a rerun. In replaying the journey, I noticed some commonalities: my faith is constant, my faith is the daily bread that sustains me, choices, commitment and courage are attributes intertwined with my faith. Faith can be difficult to understand and to embrace because it requires me to believe in what I cannot yet see, and one of my favorite reflections is that faith is a demonstration of worship to God.

As I share these five commonalities of faith in my life, I want to be clear that I am not a Christian theologian. I am simply and humbly sharing my personal thoughts regarding what stands out for me as I reflect on my walk-in faith.

One of my earliest recollections of walking in faith was when the entire department where I worked was suddenly eliminated. It was an international company, with employees across the globe and with a recognized global brand. The department I was in, was to be a 'test run' that didn't work out as planned. When the department was eliminated, I was notified that I had 30 days to post for other roles in the company. Recommendations from department leads would be a plus. The drill was that if within 30 days I had not secured a job internally, I would have the opportunity to accept a severance package. It was one of the darkest periods of my professional career. I remember asking myself…how in the world can you expect your manager to put in a good word for you when the reporting relationship was so strained. I was also facing a difficult financial situation. A fog had entered my life and for a moment I could not see through this fog. I remember crying, crying and crying for hours that day.

Just before I went to sleep that I night I had a conversation with God. I reminded him that I had accepted that job because I believed He wanted me there. I went on to tell Him that if He had allowed my job to be eliminated it was because He had something better. I poured my heart and soul out to Him with so many things that I reminded Him of that night. In ending my cry to Him, I remember telling Him that I was scared and that I did not know what His plan for me was but that I guess that was FAITH. Faith is not being able to see where He was taking me but trusting that it would all work out for my good. If for whatever reason His plan for me was not to find another job, I needed Him to teach me how to find peace with it all. Those 30 days were not easy. Zero interviews and zero leads.

The morning of day 30 arrived. I can see myself that morning on my knees, feeling exhausted spiritually. Somehow, I managed the courage to pray something to the effect of, "Father, this is the day. I don't know what you have planned on how this will end. What I do know is that you have until 3:00PM ET today to make your will with my situation known. I have done everything I can to stand in faith. Please remember that I am scared, and I don't know what to do. I only have you to rely on." I ended praying the Our Father. A few minutes before 3:00PM ET, the head of human resources called me into his office to tell me that a colleague I had worked with on a special project had just announced his retirement and strongly suggested that I be placed in the role. I accepted the position. The role was my springboard to an incredible career. Over the course of the next 15 years I would find myself reporting to the C Suite in a variety of industries and working in 13 countries. This opportunity was ultimately a rich and fulfilling experience and blessing.

My experiences have taught me that FAITH is not just believing in what God can do. It is also worshiping God with actions. Faith is also performing actions that send messages to others that they are loved by God.

GEM SIX

EMPATHY

"The great gift of human beings is that we have the power of empathy."
Meryl Streep ~ Actress

When I think of the word empathy (being able to understand and share the feelings of others)[8], the other word that comes to mind is sympathy- the perception, understanding, and reaction to the distress or need of another[9]. In most cases empathy and sympathy works together. Having empathy allows one to put him/herself in someone else's shoes while being aware of and sensitive to their feelings. Having empathy facilitates your ability to help others. In order to demonstrate empathy effectively, you have to put aside your viewpoint and try to see things through the lens of the other individual. When you do this, you will realize that other people most likely are not being evil, unkind, stubborn, or unreasonable; however, they are probably just reacting to the situation with the knowledge they have. Developing an empathic approach toward individuals is perhaps one of the most significant efforts you can make toward improving your people skills. If you take the time to understand others, they will probably want to understand you also.

Someone lacking empathy can be characterized as cold, with no feeling or human connection. I always try to avoid just giving "no" as an answer without additional reasoning and communication with the individual making the request. I intentionally add supplemental content and communication because I fear being misunderstood and labeled unempathetic. Empathy is one of the most used words when I talk about my gems and how I journey through Corporate America and life. Empathy was something that I felt was lacking in my leaders and I honestly believe that it wasn't because people wanted to be mean spirted but they just could not picture themselves in my shoes. Also, because of the industry that I was in and the environment, most of my leaders and colleagues could not empathize with me because their paths were so different from mine in many ways, often including their races, ethnicities, and gender.

Many of these individuals tried to display empathy however it was short lived because they never walked in my shoe. Feeling this lack of empathy in my work life strengthened my commitment to be there for others. Demonstrating this gem was a priority for me because I yearned for someone to show me empathy during my early professional career, from a genuine and honest place, not false or condescending.

I was fortunate that a young woman from South America was on my team, and her husband was also from South America but from a different region. They wanted their daughter who was born in America to spend the summer in Colombia, immersed in the culture and spending quality time with her dad's family. She grew homesick and began calling her mom at work five to six times per day crying. Plain and simple, she wanted to come home.

The experience was traumatic for her daughter. One day my employee came into my office, exclaiming, "Jackie, what can I do? My daughter is unhappy. I don't know what I'm going to do." She asked me a couple of times if I would brainstorm ideas with her or give her my opinion as to what I would do in this situation. As a mother with my own daughters I felt her concern so I stopped what I was doing as empathy kicked in. I knew that she could not function and do her work well with her mind distracted on her daughter, this was my opportunity to see things through her eyes.

I responded, "We are a global company. Do we have an office in Colombia?" She responded, "Yes" I said, "You are going to pack a suitcase, book a flight, and work from there." She was overjoyed that I did that for her and she spent the entire summer in Colombia. All parties involved were happy. The employee was much more productive there than she would have been had she remained in America. An additional bonus was meeting and working with our Colombian colleagues. Sometimes you can do things out of empathy and it can work out well or even better than expected. Do not be afraid or hold back when it comes to showing empathy, remember, place yourself in that person's situation and envision how you would feel if it were you. Many times, when we stop to do this we react differently because the act of exercising empathy brings the matter close to home.

I employ three key steps to demonstrate empathy effectively. The first step is: Listen to the individual, don't just hear them. Listening requires hearing the unspoken words. When we are working with people, we tend not to listen as deeply as we should. I do that a lot. Take the extra time to demonstrate patience when listening, especially if that person is from a different culture. You really do need to listen and read between the lines of what the person is saying because frequently the important points are missed. In my formative career years there was not a lot of listening going on. Of course, I had a thicker accent and still do to this day, so my pronunciation of words were sometimes different. Conversations often required patience on my part and acceptance of my accent by others.

The second step: Ask probing questions. What can I do? How can I be supportive of you? In most cases the answer is usually, "I don't know." Sometimes you will get to the crux of the matter by asking these probing questions. At times we don't know what we need or how we want the outcome of the situation to be, but with a few probing questions we can reach a solution. This often informs the employee that you have a genuine interest in their situation.

The third step: Provide a few solutions you think would work. It might not be ideal but the employee will see that you are genuinely trying to provide some assistance and that goes a long way toward retaining that individual. Together you both can brainstorm your way to a workable solution. Showing empathy to someone who is struggling because of poor decisions they may have made can make a real difference in that person's life and those connected to them. Although their situation is due to their own choices and they are now facing the repercussions, we should not become desensitized to the individual. For example, someone who is terminated from a job because of poor performance. This could result from over stating their qualifications, suspending all judgements, I would lift that individual by demonstrating empathy.

I recall working with a leader who would schedule 7:00AM staff meetings. Most of the team members were male. Three team members, including myself, were female. Meeting at 7:00AM was not a big deal for the men but was a major issue for the women who were also mothers. As mothers we walked our children to the bus stop. There was no way we could make sure our children were safely on the school bus and also make a 7:00AM staff meeting. None of the women wanted to address this. I, however, took the initiative to address this concern with our manager. Once I brought it to his attention, he quickly demonstrated empathy by changing the meeting time to accommodate us. At times, we have to bring things to people's attention. In this instance our manager was totally unaware of our situation. The moment we addressed it, he responded positively. Demonstrating empathy requires you to be able to communicate and be a good listener.

Gem Takeaways:

- Patience is required to exercise empathy.
- Work on your listening skills, we all have room for improvement.
- Just because someone is vastly different from you does not mean you cannot envision yourself in their situation
- It doesn't cost anything to help someone, most of the time it's just empathizing.
- "If you can help somebody, then your living will not be in vain[10]."

FIRST LADY ERICA HINES
JAMAICA

Eliot Congregational Church of Roxbury

───────◆───────

When I think of the word "Empathy", I think of compassion with understanding. Empathy is the ability to show sincere concern not only for those you care for and love, but for anyone that struggles or suffers. The act of "Empathy" allows a person that is broken, hurting, depressed, or just in need of basic care, to feel that someone is standing beside them and supporting them without judgment. Psalm 46 tells us that God is a very present help. Empathy allows us to be used by God in such a way that our presence serves as an extension of His compassion. It is with "Empathy" that I am able to not only assist my husband as a pastor, but to live as an example for my children, extended family, lead as a Director for an energy company and serve a congregation and community as a First Lady and concerned citizen.

I first met Jackie Glenn when I was a newlywed, with a newborn and a new career. Overwhelmed and experiencing the growing pains of life, like the proverbial big sister, Jackie Glenn came along and took me under her wing. As part of our becoming acquainted, Jackie introduced me to the business of Mary Kay and the camaraderie of sisters who were involved. I met a host of professional, accomplished, beautiful, black ladies. It was like a sorority of sisters all just like Jackie. While my young marriage and early career goals prohibited my full involvement, the networking, friendships and professional insight that I developed would stay with me for years to come.

As a young African American female managing the demands of family, vocation, and education; my friendship with Jackie was invaluable. She was always right there to not only encourage me through those challenging moments but also serve as my mentor. As an experienced Human Resources professional, she showed me firsthand how to navigate my way through necessary processes and protocols to ensure that I could take needed time off, without losing my job.

As a wife and mother, herself, Jackie and her husband fully availed themselves to my husband and me without reservation. I will always remember during the early nineties, Jackie was pregnant with her second daughter and I never imagined a sister could look so impeccable even while pregnant. In typical Big Sister fashion, while expecting my second daughter, Jackie passed along her beautiful maternity dresses; one, in particular, was a tent style, gold, and black dress. Not only knowing that my mentor spent a fortune for the outfits, but actually wearing the same dress gave me a real boost of confidence. I felt Jackie had handed me her mantle like Elijah to Elisha in the Old Testament. I still have a picture in one of the dresses where I'm attempting to replicate the same pose I saw Jackie assume at a holiday event.

On other occasions when I just needed to get away and unable to afford it, Jackie would intervene and help me book a flight and hotel. She understood how important it was just to get away, take a break, regroup and then come back to the demands of work and day to day life. She looked out for my family and I just as if we were her own. In many ways she was more than a big sister, she was a protector. Jackie was quite aware that the American Dream did not come easy especially when you are young, black, and female. Jackie knew what it meant to work hard to pursue your dreams, and she was right there to help me and my family do the same. These were definitely Jackie's strengths from day one, and she remains the same kind and compassionate person to date.

Jackie has always been an upbeat and positive influence in the lives of so many. I can recall her going through her own challenges. Yet, in light of losing her brother and mom, somehow, she was still this energetic and caring person towards me and others. Over the years when I later relocated to New York and then Chicago, Jackie maintained our friendship, staying in touch and continuously caring for me. My sister would even visit with us when we lived in Chicago; despite the distance, she was always right there.

From 1990 right up to this very day, I have both witnessed and experienced Jackie being a role model for so many. I am convinced that she has given so much, and in return, God continues to bless her and her lovely family in so many ways. Jackie is not just blessed, but she is indeed a blessing. She is a spiritually grounded, loving, professional, proud Christian Black woman. So often family, friends, colleagues, and acquaintances upon discovering she is my dear friend, sister, and mentor will ask me, "Can I meet with her?" My usual response is to let them know that she is a very busy lady, but I am sure that when she has the opportunity, she will. While I often want to keep her all to myself, I know that she is the type of person who has a passion and desire to give back, and not just pull someone up, but alongside her. How fitting that she has decided to share and tell her story of how she both lifts and climbs.

My dear sister, Mrs. Jackie Glenn, thank you for being a world changer! Thank you for being my Big Sister and Mentor. Thank you for being someone who inspires so many, but especially for being our sisters, a confident woman of significant influence. Jackie, you have motivated and still motivate both the young and seasoned sister you've encountered along the way. I am blessed to know you. Thank you for all you have done and continue to do. Thank God for bringing you into my life as someone who will always mean so much to me. Thank you for just being you!

GEM SEVEN

FLEXIBILITY

"*What is malleable is always superior to that which is immovable.
This is the principle of controlling things by going along
with them, of mastery through adaptation.*"

Lao Tzu ~ Philosopher

Flexibility means the ability to pivot, not necessarily going wherever the wind blows. It means not being too rigid, but rather the ability to be fluid. Flexibility is the capacity to work with what life throws your way without being labeled a pushover or a troublemaker. This particular gem is an important quality for a good leader, a good mentor and an all-around good person because it allows an individual to see both sides of the coin. There has to be a balance between being flexible and being a "yes person." I do believe that when you are flexible, it yields great results in many areas, whether you are in the workplace, school or volunteering.

When hiring talent, I look for the best and the brightest, those who can make a difference and deliver results. It is one thing to hire someone, but it take hard work to retain them. In some cases, we lose talent because of inflexibility, not willing to bend on one's position. Losing talent because of inflexibility is losing money. Time and money spent developing these individuals is wasted if they leave because differences could not be resolved.

Selfishly, I always look at ways I can be flexible in working with everyone, especially the talented ones who work for and with me. I realize that being flexible works out better for me in the end and everyone wins. My hiring preference is and individual who is adaptable and readily embrace changes. My unconventional approach, when it comes to hiring qualifications has generated big wins for me over time. As long as the applicant is well rounded, a quick study and flexible I am not overly focused on the job description, especially for certain roles.

I can train a person on most jobs and skillsets if they are willing and adaptable. I once had an employee take a position with me whose husband, at about the same time, received a fellowship to pursue his doctorate in another state. This was a great opportunity for her husband and ultimately her family. Upon accepting the position with me she and her husband made the decision that she would remain in state and he would move. Months into her role she became pregnant and informed me early in the pregnancy so we could agree on the go forward plan. I appreciated her proactive approach in sharing because dialogue and conversation are key tenants to flexibility.

As her due date drew closer she wanted to know what my thought was when she got to her eight month. I was flexible and open enough to ask her what she needed from me to make this work for her and the company. She was ready to join her husband. Underscoring the need for one hundred percent in her performance and setting clear expectations and I left no gray areas or cause for assumptions. I told her that I expected her to be on team calls and reachable for questions, etc. I did not put a roadmap in front of her because I wanted her to own it and come up with how she was going to get this done efficiently.

As a technology company we had all of the equipment and resources to make the remote connection work. My employee happily relocated and worked remotely after her maternity leave. She did that for about two years until her husband was finished with his fellowship and then they moved back in state and she worked from the office. She was one of my best employee and had I not demonstrated flexibility I would have lost a great talent.

She modeled the remote working situation with such precision that I asked her to write a guide on how to work remotely. After that experience, I would let her work remotely anytime she asked because she had proven herself. There are managers who would deny a request to work remotely because they believe being in the office s most productive. I discovered being present in the office does not mean you are working hard.

There are times and professions when being flexible with remote work is not feasible. For example, the physical presence of nurses, doctors and/or patient care providers are required to be in hospital or clinical settings. Flexibility is demonstrated in many different ways. Managers who make it clear they are willing to be flexible when different situations arise, are working toward creating work environments that are open to greater productivity. Inject flexibility whenever and wherever you can, especially with an employee who is a rock star. When exercising this gem one must be aware of the progress on all project and if signs are observed that the employee is taking advantage of the situation, a conversation needs to take place immediately. Frequent check point and assessments are invaluable tools to determine if expectations need to be reinforced.

Flexibility does not only apply to a working relationship but in all interactions both personal and professional. Unseen opportunities arise when we are flexible allowing us to move beyond our usual way of thinking and into creative options. Flexibility also gives us a host of ways to view situations and opens us up to a great new world of possibilities. Our ability to be flexible is not meant to give anyone the opportunity to walk all over us, but our flexibility is meant to allow us to be open and caring.

There are so many ways to think, feel and go about our lives. Some of us are at home with our families trying to figure out what to make for dinner. Some of us are at school working on a project team. Others are in organizations brainstorming and innovating, while some of us are in the boardroom determining future direction and strategy. Our entrepreneur friends are trying to make their way with valued and vibrant business models. Being flexible and open to all ideas, thoughts and processes will always be a great way to go. Keep in mind that although you are being flexible it doesn't mean you are going to just roll over and accept everything, but that you will always listen and be as flexible as possible.

Gem Takeaways:

- Flexibility does not mean being a pushover.
- Mastering the competency of being flexible will enhance your career or business.
- There are times when not being flexible is a good thing.
- Being a good listener is a good start to being flexible.
- Being flexible opens you to different ways of thinking.

PATRICIA FLORISSI
BRAZIL

Vice President & Global Chief Technology Officer

———————◆———————

I am originally from Recife, Pernambuco, located in the poor northeast region of Brazil. My husband and I met in college, at the Federal University of Pernambuco, and we started dating during the second year of our computer science undergraduate course. At the time, Brazil was a closed country and the only way to further expand our knowledge in the area was by studying abroad. The process to do so was clear: students needed to have completed an undergraduate degree and be pursuing a master's degree before applying. We started our master's in January 1988, a program that typically took 2 ½ years to complete. The year of 1989 was a presidential election year in Brazil and the most popular candidate at the time vowed to end the overseas program should he be elected. My husband and I decided to work extra hard to finish our master's degree in 1 ½ year and leave to study abroad in September 1989, before the elections. As fate would have it, the most popular candidate won, inaugurated in January 1990 and put severe constraints in the program. We would not have come to the United States had we not left in 1989. Seizing the moment represents our first element of flexibility.

We applied to many universities but Columbia University in New York City was the first that accepted both my husband and me, and it was really important for us to be together. Accepting constraints to be together represents our second element of flexibility. It took us six years to complete our Ph.D., after which we decided to return to Brazil with the expectation to live the rest of our lives in Brazil and raise our family there. However, within five weeks of arriving in Brazil, my mother passed away and my husband got sick, requiring a treatment not available in Brazil at the time. Our Ph.D. advisor invited us back to the US. I would work for a start-up company he had founded and my husband would work for Columbia University with him as a research assistant. Dramatically shifting lifetime planning represented our third element of flexibility.

The start-up environment in the United States, especially in Computer Science and in the late 1990s, was hectic. Roles and responsibilities were not defined, let alone understood. I absolutely did everything they asked me to do on the job. I didn't say no to anything I was asked to do, and in employing that mindset, I was able to expand my areas of learning. I touched all elements of the business. Humbly adjusting to the needs of the business represented my fourth element of flexibility.

At the start-up, I was constantly stretching myself, mentally and physically. Only a couple of months in, I was asked to teach a one week course on the methodology and on the software the company was developing. I had to learn the course over a weekend in order to teach it on Monday. But once I mastered the course, I was then asked to travel constantly to teach it in the United States and in Europe, which gave me reach to a diverse set of customers. Being always ready to accept challenges and interpreting them as development opportunities represented my fifth element of flexibility.

As time went on, the start-up was acquired by EMC. When EMC executives asked what I wanted to do next, everyone knew I dreamed of pursuing an MBA degree to bring a business acumen to my technical background. I was given the opportunity to pursue a two year executive MBA and, once again, I seized the moment. Having an MBA opened opportunities on the more strategic side of the business. I was asked to lead a strategic initiative on Governance, Risk and Compliance (GRC). Even though I was not familiar with the area, I again accepted the challenge. Working with GRC gave me exposure to sales, which led to an opportunity to become the Chief Technology Officer (CTO) for Sales. It's important to note that the last two or three jobs were not positions that existed before hand but were positions that were created when I came. I'm always telling others that sometimes your ideal job is not out there but you have to be available to transform yourself and be agile enough to take every opportunity that presents itself and work with what is presented to you. Being ready to sail uncharted seas represented my sixth element of flexibility.

In essence, for me, you have to be flexible or die. I was on a call the other day, and I was talking to our sales force and asking them what is their biggest challenge? And I would say four out of five said the biggest problem that they have is that they are trying to help their customers go through a digital transformation and their customers are transforming themselves as they go through the process. So we went through the process from A to Z that our customers are going through. One week, our sales team works with a customers' team members and then, a couple of weeks after, the customer has experienced a transformation of not only roles but also of personnel.

Two weeks later, everybody had a different role and the organizational structure is different and there are different people we have to educate and it speaks to lives being changed for the better. This experience is not only unique to Dell EMC but everywhere you go this transformation is occurring and people are being forced to reinvent themselves. We no longer have a steady business model, or business practices but it's a continuous learning process and you have to be flexible to keep up. We must stay in tuned and 'present' in our ever-changing landscape. Often, we think we are doing great and all is well, when this could not be further from the truth. Suddenly, our job disappears and we are no longer relevant or needed.

Being paranoid about the vulnerability of our careers, believing we are entitled to nothing, but must fight and thrive at every step of the way, represents my seventh element of flexibility.

GEM EIGHT

INTEGRITY

———————————◆———————————

*"The qualities of a great man are vision, integrity, courage,
understanding, the power of articulation, and profundity of character."*

Dwight Eisenhower, American Army General
& 34th President of the United States

Integrity is a quality that I pride myself on and practice daily. My personality should be consistent with who I am on a regular basis. Even when it does not seem to be the popular thing to do, practicing integrity always pays off.

I regard the Integrity gem as foundational, a resource to ground and calibrate you when you face difficult decisions. One example of using the Integrity gem happened early in my career of as Chief Diversity Officer. I had several employees in the LGBTQ (Lesbian, Gay, Bisexual Transgender and Queer) community approach me asking to form an Employee Resource Group. The company already had other resource groups in place, but not one with a mission centered on our LGBT employees and issues of importance to them, I gave the hopeful organizers direction and how to put a proposal together for submission. Once that was completed, the next step was for me to present it to my leadership team for approval. I took it to my manager whose immediate response was "the company is not ready." I was told to hold off on presenting it to the broader leadership team. While disappointed, I decided to use this "holding off" time to research and gather data and evidence showing why the LGBT Resource Group made sense, as well as the best practices that other leading companies – and competitors for our talent -- were adopting and implementing.

As time went by the LGBT group continued to ask me about the progress on their proposal. During these conversations, I began to have an almost physical reaction that I now recognize as the Integrity gem in action. When your integrity is compromised, you can actually feel the reaction in your body, as well as the deflation of your spirit. The best remedy for this is to listen to what is happening in your mind, body and spirit, and then take action. Feeling that my integrity was at risk, I wanted to at least bring the request to our full leadership team and hear their decision and rationale I only needed to wait a few weeks before the opportunity arrived. Although I was told by my manager that the company "was not ready," I decided to take the risk, bring it up and ask for forgiveness later.

I began the conservation with the leadership team by acknowledging to my manager that I was not being insubordinate by raising the request, but I felt that my integrity was at stake. I had made a promise and my reputation was based on the value of my word. I then presented the proposal and outlined the importance of being inclusive and being seen as leader in our industry. I drew confidence in the strength of the proposal, the evidence I had put together, and the implications for employee retention, engagement and performance. Within the hour, I was given the green light to move forward with the launch of our LGBTQ Employee Resource Group. It all started with a promise, delivered by integrity.

A few years later, I could feel my internal Integrity monitor go off once again, but this time it was tied to a feeling of pride and honor. I had just received notification that we were awarded a perfect score on the Corporate Equality Index, a widely respected indicator of being an inclusive company for LGBTQ colleagues. This annual award, created by an American civil rights and advocacy organization called the Human Rights Campaign, is built on a rigorous set of measurements that examine the policies, practices and actions that drive workplace equality. It is not an easy designation to earn, and even more difficult to maintain. During my tenure, we earned a perfect score for multiple years. We welcomed members of our executive team and our Board of Directors to march in an LGBTQ Pride Parade. Members of the LGBTQ resource group became visible and respected for bringing their whole and authentic selves to work. Our work in this area earned the company significant external recognition for efforts such as our internal guide and planning for transgender colleagues who were returning to work with a new gender identity.

Speaking to the Associated Press about our work in this area, I again felt the power of the Integrity that our company was now extending to the world. When I would travel to parts of the world where LGBTQ people face discrimination or even criminal prosecution, I had discussions about our values as a global organization, and though I could not instantly change outdated laws and mindsets, I could always set the expectation of how people would be treated as a member of our global team. For some of the colleagues I met on my travels, it was deeply gratifying and concerning that work was one of the safest places they could be.

Like all of the gems that I recommend, it is always gratifying to have their value increase over time. My Integrity gem would go on to serve me well many years later, when I was asked by a an enthusiastic group of employees if they could start an Employee Resource Group for people of various faiths. The idea was to be able to have an open forum at work to explore various beliefs, in an inclusive and supportive environment. Space would be made available for meetings and discussions, and gatherings would be open to everyone, regardless of where they were on their individual faith journey. My earlier experience advising corporate leaders on the topic of sexuality and gender identity was now needed to navigate something equally intrinsic and personal. As I listened to the objections and concerns of how faith was not somewhere we wanted to go, the Integrity gem took on a new light. When I attended the launch of our Faith Employee Resource Group and looked at the diversity of beliefs and backgrounds on the appreciative faces in front of me, I knew once again that Integrity rises above fear. It is something I never forget.

Gem Takeaways:

- Build the narrative to support your case, put data and evidence into compelling stories that will move others to action.
- Be prepared to defend your ideas and keep your promises.
- Honor the responsibility of speaking for others who cannot be heard.
- Even under fire and persecution stay true to yourself.

DR. JEAN-BERNARD CHARLES
HAITI

Ophthalmologist

———————————◆◀———————————

My name is Jean-Bernard Charles. I was born in Haiti and I first travelled to America when I was about 11 years old for a summer vacation. Over the ensuing years I traveled back and forth until my eldest brother emigrated to attend Northeastern University. I was 14 when my entire family decided to relocate permanently. From that point on, I dedicated myself to my academic studies while attending boarding school in Montreal, Canada followed by preparatory school in Boston to improve my proficiency in American English and to prepare me to attend college in Boston. While at Boston University, I obtained my first degree and went on to medical school. During that time, I took a year off from medical training to attend the Fletcher School of Law and Diplomacy at Tufts University. Following medical school, I went on to postgraduate studies in ophthalmology at King-Drew Medical Center in Los Angeles, California, after which I returned to the Boston area for fellowship training at the Joslin Diabetes Center.

My family still lived in Boston, so I established a clinical practice in the urban community where my professional skills could be best put to use. I was the only Haitian ophthalmologist in the Boston area for the last 20 years and one of only four practicing black ophthalmologists for over 12 years. About 10 years into the practice, I decided to pursue additional training in public health and in clinical research. I obtained a master's degree in Public Health from the Harvard School of Public

Health. Recognizing anew that my first love was really to take care of patients, I returned to clinical practice with a deeper awareness and the larger perspective of public health. Over the years, the practice has evolved into a thriving multicultural practice comprising sizable cohorts of African Americans, Vietnamese and Caribbean patients. It's a practice in which many patients have developed a vested interest and take personal pride in their experience and their care.

Regarding the notion of integrity, its meaning and basis in my own life, my immigrant experience and my professional career have served as the foundation that sustained and fueled my sense of integrity and the pursuit thereof. In the perennial search for self-identity and authenticity, I have come to define the meaning of integrity as being true to myself and honoring the components of my complete heritage in every aspect of my life.

My integrity as a healthcare provider allows authentic communication with my patients regardless of their ethnicity whether of Vietnamese, Caribbean, or American backgrounds. It doesn't matter. The clinical and scientific expertise of doctoring can then be exercised upon a foundation of trust and mutual respect. This approach to practicing is what gives meaning to the word integrity for me at the end of a day's work, the integrity of my service, the integrity of my practice.

When I think deeply of integrity, the first thing which comes to mind is that I have to know who I am, by probing the depth and breadth of my inner world, by being introspective. I must be the observer of my own consciousness, my own world, my own life, my own activities and my own behavior. I must always be sensitive and aware of what I am doing as if I am standing beside myself, watching myself. But in order to do that, I, of necessity, need to divest myself from myself, and place myself in the position of observer monitoring and analyzing my feelings, my thoughts and actions. Then, the secondary exercise that follows this awareness is to engage myself as the inner physician, philosopher or counselor who can heal and resolve my inner conflicts by persuasive logic and reassuring wisdom, or as the inner surgeon who can excise and drain the tumors and abscesses of maladaptive biases, selfish motives, and recurring momentums of fear once they get exposed by the searchlight of self-introspection.

As a doctor, one's ability to push aside the burdens of conflicted and unresolved feelings and thoughts in order to better serve and address the issues and needs of others is what defines integrity for me. The privilege of serving others through medical practice becomes an ongoing inner process of self-refinement of one's humanity that never ends. This integrity, therefore, can be compromised not only by external forces that undermine one's ability to embrace and actualize who one truly is, but also by any internal condition and state of consciousness lacking in peace and quietude within one's own being and one's own consciousness. If I were to codify and share the wisdom I gleaned from my immigrant life experience, I would say, "First and foremost quiet your mind and pursue peace with yourself. Be aware of what's going on inside of you, of your motives, and resolve to make changes within, wherever you deem necessary. Through that process, develop the capacity to share and serve in such a way that you control and authenticate your service free from the influence of whatever unresolved conditions or challenges that are currently preoccupying your life."

In that manner, you would develop the capacity to bridge any cultural differences, navigate through any social conundrums, and contribute positively to the wellbeing of a society that has welcomed you as an immigrant in the midst. These actions result in an inner sense of gratitude, a calmness of spirit, and an underlying equanimity founded upon an ever expanding and defining sense of self-awareness. Within the context of this temperate disposition and openness, I endeavor to engage in my daily activities, navigate life's myriad challenges to learn their lessons, and interact with others as authentically as I am able, as healthcare provider, as friend, as co-worker, or as fellow citizen in a personal search for understanding and common ground. Such is the integrity and authenticity for which I yearn and to which I endeavor to honor in my life as an immigrant and as a fellow human being.

AYMAN YOUSSEF
BEIRUT

Owner of Aroma Group

———————◆———————

I came to the United States in 1991. Two of my brothers arrived before me, in 1978. We chose to relocate to this country by obtaining our permanent residency. We went to school and after graduating we got several side jobs, starting in Detroit, Michigan. Later we moved to Toledo, Ohio and then I moved to Florida. I lived between these three states for approximately seven years. During that time, I worked many jobs, from restaurants to grocery stores, gas stations, and a car company that made car parts for GM. I did almost every type of job.

While in Florida I tried to start my own business, but it was very tough. I worked three different jobs then. I worked at the Ritz Carlton Hotel from 5:00PM until 11:00PM and ran my own business from 8:00AM until 4:00PM. I did that for three years and started saving more money. Eventually my business started getting better, so I quit my extra jobs.

Our parents raised us to be kind and show respect to all human beings. We never noticed the differences between types of people. We recognized each person as human. We did not even know much about other religions, we just treated everyone as our friend. These principles came with me when I migrated to the United States.

I had a great reputation regarding my work ethic. Everyone wanted me to run his/her store because of my honesty and hard work. I did not believe in standing around and doing nothing. If my assigned duties were completed, I looked for something else to do even if that job was not a part of my duties. My business grew rapidly because of my hard work and dedication. I treated people the way I wanted to be treated. I never lied, so if I made a mistake with a customer I would call and make it right. One of the things that I learned from my dad was that if you ever wanted to say something to someone, try it on yourself first.

I taught my subcontractors/installers to first respect the homes where they were working: do not open the refrigerator because this is not their house, do not even take a bottle of water or a Coke. You are there to work. Secondly, you are working for me so, please follow my instructions and direction because I am responsible for this job/project. I have a reputation to live up to and that is "Ayman doesn't lie." So, they learned from my principles, that if they're working with me, they are not to go through the owner's things and not to be disrespectful. I've gained some respect from them; they respect what I do and how I serve people. I like to do the job right. That for me is integrity.

Because I have a great reputation, a carpet store owner gave our mosque free carpet. Additionally, because we have developed a relationship, I am now able to run a tab of up to $16,000. I have an honest reputation and they trust me. I believe that one should be honest and do the right thing, don't cut corners. If you cut corners, you're not going to last in this field too long. If you lie it will catch up with you sooner or later. So, we were immigrants and we came to this country. I love this land and how it opened its arms for all of us and gave us an opportunity to achieve a dream we could never achieve in our own country. I consider this my country now. There are some people who abuse the system a lot and it bothers me sometimes. I am an advocate for being trustworthy and honest and living by my integrity because it goes a long way.

GEM NINE

RESILIENCE

---◆---

"You may have to fight a battle more than once to win it."
Margaret Thatcher ~ Former British Prime Minister

Have you ever read a novel you just could not put down? Did it describe how a person fell into a ditch and eventually dragged themselves out? Spending time in the ditch allows you to build character and tenacity that is needed to get out of your situation. For me resilience is a person sitting in that space of uncomfortableness waiting, not forever, but giving themselves some time to bounce back. This space never feels good because most people don't like adversity, conflict or problems. The moment these situations arise many people run or if they stay, they do it kicking and screaming. Resilience is the ability to stay put even when it does not feel good. In other words, you have to stay uncomfortable until you become comfortable.

Resilience is the ability to bounce back, to pick yourself up when you fall, to try again and never give up until you can truly say you gave it your all. It is having the capability to sit still and stay patient in the hot seat even if it's burning your booty. For most people it is conventional to run when the going gets rough. They give up and throw in the towel. These tough life lessons are invaluable because it is in the midst of being resilient that you realize the learning. In this space one acquires the life experiences beyond that is conveyed through traditional learning. Staying in unfavorable situations gives you knowledge and strategy that can lift others in their journey to becoming resilient.

An example of how I used resilience occurred during a situation where my boss talked me into taking a certain role then for some reason she became indifferent towards me but loved my work. She did everything within her power to stunt my career growth even though the role I was in qualified me for a promotion equivalent to my peers. She consistently promoted others who were less experienced and were not half as skilled and qualified. This continued year after year and I kept waiting and asking if there was anything I needed to do differently, and she always responded "no."

I knew this was one of those situations where I had to maintain my resilience in the midst of this trying circumstance. At this point, encouraging myself to stay strong and wait was my approach. When meeting with my manager I would ask what I should work on and where I could improve in my leadership style. I remained very proactive with my development and soliciting feedback. Hearing the word feedback can make one become defensive, especially if it is negative. Resilience will allow you to embrace the feedback and do whatever is necessary to make improvements.

In requesting feedback, I demonstrated to my manager that I heard her and was looking forward to her partnering with me for a resolution. This in turn encouraged her to provide me an executive coach which I completely supported. Throughout the process, I remained true to myself. I continued to be fair and respectful to everyone I came in contact with. A large piece of demonstrating resilience is being true to who you are and your beliefs. Here is a story of the resilience gem at work. One day, when I was feeling down over another situation of being passed over and marginalized, I bumped into the leader of our department as I walked down the hall. She stopped and asked, "Jackie, how are you doing?" I replied, "I am sure you know how I am doing." She said, "There are always two sides to every story. Why don't you come see me?" I said, "Oh, sure." In my internal voice, I said, "Yeah, right, you are never going to let me come see you." When I returned to my office I saw that she had already sent me a meeting invite.

In hindsight this woman believed and trusted my integrity and was not swayed by what others might be saying about me.

As I prepared to go meet with her, I remember having a conversation with my husband regarding what I was going to say. At this point, I was also struggling after discovering I was making significantly less than my peers' direct reports. There were other pressing concerns that did not put me in the ideal frame of mind to go meet with my manager's manager. I had to remind myself of who I was, why I was doing this and to stay true to my values.

My husband encouraged me to be calm and not allow my emotions to fuel the conversation. I prepared four key questions that would help me to steer the dialogue in a positive direction, with the hope of getting a positive outcome. The questions were:

- Why am I not a vice president?
- What do I have to do to get there?
- Why am I making significantly less than my peers' direct reports?
- Do you have any feedback for me?

After asking my questions I stayed silent and waited for her to respond, I was determined not to get carried away with excessive talking. She appeared stunned and shocked by my disclosure.

After a few moments of contemplation, she looked at me, shook her head and said, "Jackie I don't have the answers to those questions. But I promise you, I am going to get the answers and I will come back to you." Yes, I was very nervous, but I knew it would be really important for me to use this opportunity to get answers to my questions while remaining positive. My mom always said, "To thine own self be true"[10] (William Shakespeare)." When you have a chance for a one on one with your leader, preparation is critically important, and you have to strike while the iron is hot. Know what you are going in to say and why, do your research and know the facts, do not offer second hand information that cannot be verified. Be transparent and acknowledge that you know the narrative of how others may be perceiving you.

A few months later I got a call from the leader informing me that I had been promoted and that she would also fix the salary issue. Had I not employed the gem of maintaining my resilience even when it appeared everyone and everything was against me, I would not have gotten this positive outcome. I boldly stepped into that conversation and asked for what I wanted with respect and integrity. I honestly do not think I would have gotten promoted or received a salary remediation if I had not advocated for myself. Your resilience is the only leg you have to stand on when it seems everything else has been stripped from you. This gem can be used in every area of your life, whether it is working for a corporation, being an entrepreneur or in a personal situation. Maintaining your resilience is always the winning route to take.

<u>Gem Takeaways:</u>

- Get comfortable with growing, stretching and demonstrating resilience in thought and ideas.
- Remember things always work out the way they are supposed to.
- Resilience is the ability to stay put when it does not feel good, you have to stay uncomfortable until you become comfortable.
- Understand your purpose or reason for being resilient.
- Being resilient requires you know your facts and do your research.
- See your situations as opportunities to develop resilience.

MARIA DEFATIMA BARROS, RN, MSN
CAPE VERDE

Registered Nurse

I was born on Cape Verde Island a former Portuguese Colony and my maternal grandparents first came to America in 1915. They like with many other "Portuguese" came on the packed ships to New Bedford Massachusetts in search of the American dream. My grandfather worked picking cranberries in Mass and on the railroad in Connecticut. During the depression their situation was bad so they returned to Cape Verde.

My grandparents purchased lots of land on the Island of Santo Antao. They had workers making and selling Grougue (rum).fruits and vegetable were sold to the other islands. My family were considered affluent. They were descendants of Moroccan Jews, Portuguese, Indians, and British like most former Colonial Islands. A mix of races, cultures and ethnicity and I find it interesting that they do not mention Africans.

A severe drought lead to the famine of 1950. My grandfather began selling parcels of land. He took his youngest teenage son and left for Argentina. They never returned to Cape Verde. My grandmother stayed with five children. Somehow she was able to care for them as well as other families that depended on her. Everyone that knew her said she fed and saved many lives during the horrible famine. My mother returned to America on 1956 in search of a better life. During that time she lived with her aunt and extended family. Being pregnant with my sister, she worked two jobs cleaning homes and as a housekeeper at a local hospital. In 1957 she sent for her husband (my stepdad) and my two year old brother.

In 1958 at the tender age of six, skinny, lonely, sickly, afraid and unable to speak English I arrived in America. I gradually noticed the different appearance from my family; my brother, baby sister, father and family were all white skinned! My mom was also much lighter than I was. I was unhappy, uncomfortable and felt misplaced in this place which was my new home. Our neighborhood was mostly Jewish and Irish where no one spoke Creole and they looked at me funny! My father worked as a bus boy at hotel in Providence. He fitted right in with Italians and learned to speak their language. After all he was Portuguese and looked like them.

Being very shy I became withdrawn. I was sickly and diagnosed with scarlet fever had to be hospitalized which seemed like forever. By the time I finally went home I had learned to speak a little English. There were no ESL (English as a Second Language) classes in the 60s. I endured my fair share of intense bullying. People did not know who a Capeverdean was. Feeling further isolated and detached because of the horrible names I was called. Both the black and white kids did not want to be my friend. My siblings along with other mixed race kids had to learn to fight learned to fight to defend ourselves and survive. Many thought I was rebellious, but I had simply reached a point in my young life that I was not going to allow anyone to put me down anymore. This was the only way I knew how to survive... I was in survival mode. This was my way of being resilient.

My mother worked two jobs and not only did she cared for her five children but she had my aunt's three daughters because my aunt was hospitalized. We had mix race children placed with us. Within 3 years of arriving in America, my parents bought a three Family house. Our extended family kept growing so eventually my mom sent for my grandmother to come help care for us. My grandmother was a wise woman and she taught me about our culture, customs and life skills. She made sure we all knew about heritage and would say " you are a mixture of White, Black, Jews and India people so hold your head high and be proud." She was adamant that we learn how to stand on our two feet and handle ourselves in any situation.

From an early age I was the one caring for the cuts and bruises of my younger siblings. I enjoyed helping even the neighborhood kids. I knew I wanted to be a doctor! I survived elementary thru high school and at the age of seventeen I was married to an older cousin in order for him to stay in this country. This was a common practice not just in our Capeverdean Community but many immigrant communities. I was an honor student and was offered scholarships to colleges. My dream was to be a good doctor. I was in an unhealthy marriage and despite criticisms from my family about getting a divorce I stuck it out until I was twenty years old. I worked as a dietary aide and was trained as a nursing assistance at a local hospital.

Being resilient about my career path I enrolled in a two year Registered Nurse program. My schedule was hectic working, going to nursing school full time and being a single mother. Thank God for my extended family! After graduating I worked on the Intensive Care, Orthopedic, Medical, Surgical and Trauma units. The only area I refused to work on was Pediatric. I had the unfortunate experience during my nursing school caring for two children with cancer. The painful testing and treatments they had to endure caused me to question my faith in our God. When asked what nugget of wisdom I can pass on regarding resiliency, I would say; be prepared, be careful, be confident, be knowledgeable, be honest and educated. You've got to defend yourself. Don't give up because one or a few people put you down because doors will open and you must be prepared. Don't let the meanness of others defeat you, just keep standing tall. Remind yourself that you know who you are. Resilience requires deliberate and intentional preparedness!

GEM TEN

TRUST

───────◆◆◆───────

"If you want people to trust you, then you have to be trustworthy."

Michelle Obama

Trust is so fundamental in everything that I do and without it nothing works for me. I know that's really a profound statement, but the trust factor in this gem is being able to rely on someone and also for you to be a reliable individual. It is the conviction that you place in others that they have your best interest at heart. There are so many applications of how and when we trust. These include trusting yourself, your decision making and trusting others. The core of any relationship, professional or personal, is trust. I find that people will go above and beyond for you when they trust you.

Trust is often connected to confidence, but for this gem I like to focus on the conviction and reliability component. As a professional who often engages in recruiting people to fill different roles, one of the competencies that is important to me is trust. I make it known during the interviewing process that everything for me is anchored on trust. I do not believe it is necessary to share all of the details of my life, but I do want to share enough to make people aware that they can trust me and that I am committed to do what is right for them. Usually I underscore the fact that I have their best interest at heart if they choose to work for me, and I expect the same in return.

Life and relationships are not perfect, so if things are not working and our relationship becomes strained, I expect communication, so we can work on what needs to be addressed. You can count on me to be trustworthy and fair because I believe that in order for trust to develop and thrive it must be a two -way street. Trust is not merely a verbal affirmation saying, "I trust you." It should be clearly demonstrated by your actions. Trust comes in many forms. An example could be how you trusted yourself and made the decision to leave your current job to take a new position that could be risky. In this case it is really trusting your judgment and your decision making skills. Sometimes trusting yourself is not only an important step in knowing who you are, but also in acknowledging your vision for your life.

I once had a good friend, or so I thought. I believed that individual was trustworthy although everyone kept telling me not to trust this person. I ignored several warnings of distrust on the individual part and continued to blindly trust. Finally, there was a major incident that had distrust written all over it. I had no recourse but to believe what I had been ignoring over the years. If something does not feel right, you must trust yourself and make a decision to identify it and stop it immediately. In this instance, I turned the prism several different ways in order to accept the fact that this person was not trustworthy.

Now that I have had time to process what happened, the lesson I have taken from this situation is, I was so focused on being a trusting friend that I missed the cues that were being displayed. Although my heart was broken, and I was sad, and disappointed; instead of assigning blame I take full responsibility for the fact that I avoided all the signs and warnings and chose to be trustworthy. Maya Angelou states, "when people show you who they are, believe them (the first time)"[14]. I would encourage everyone to watch the warning signs and not make excuses for them.

I like to give people the opportunity to build trust and if I find that I cannot trust you in the small things, then be sure I would not be able to on a larger scale. For example, be truthful about everything, even something as small as your working hours. If you are going to be late completing a project, communicate. Do not come in five minutes before the project is due to inform me you are going to be late, and act as though you were there an hour earlier to inform me. If you make a mistake, tell me and we can work together to correct it and on the flipside if I do instead of going to a third party speak to me about it with the hope that we can come to an amicable agreement. A note will suffice if face to face does not work for you.

I believe in second chances, however if trust is violated my first instinct is to withdraw myself. As it relates to the workplace, the individual might not lose his/her job, but they would no longer be in my inner circle. I will always have that third eye on the individual until they have earned that trust back. There would have to be a consistent display of trust in their words and actions. This does not happen easily because there will always be that fear that this person might do the same thing again. Trust broken is not easily regained.

In a conversation with one of my mentees she informed me that she was planning on reporting her boss for treating her badly. My response was, "Trust is a two way street, if you want your boss to trust you then you also have to demonstrate trust." This suggestion was based on my experience with another boss when he refused to promote me and blamed it on his boss. I asked him, "Are you okay with me going to speak to your boss?" Making your intentions and your next move known is also a component of trust. Talk with your manager first and if no resolution then an only then should you go to the next level. To go behind the individual's back, blindsiding them and making the situation worse, usually that does not work out in your favor because even though you might be the most brilliant, you leave your boss no recourse but to say, "You know what? That employee is brilliant but you cannot trust her." With that kind of reputation your progress becomes challenging.

It is always my intention to enter into every relationship with a sense of trust, giving everyone the benefit that they are worthy of being trusted. My name should be synonymous with trust and honesty because when I give my word I honor it. One of my leaders once said, if he wanted to hear the truth he would come to me knowing I would tell him the truth no matter the consequence.

There was a situation with an executive who I gave counsel and he did the complete opposite which caused a huge budgetary problem. Senior management asked why he was over budget and he blamed me. I was reprimanded although I told my side of the story. I continued to trust that at some point the truth would be revealed. It took a while but eventually the leader came and apologized. Sometimes you have to trust that people will do the right thing and all you have to own is your action.

Using the trust gem is always the right way to go and learning to trust others even when your trust has been broken and violated. You cannot become so paranoid that you live your life not trusting anyone. See trust as:

T-----Truthful
R-----Reliable
U-----Unify/Unity
S ----Secure
T-----Trainable

Gem Takeaways:

- Being trustworthy is a testament to your integrity.
- Walls of trust are built in tandem with those around you.
- Always enter into every situation with trust as an anchor.
- Blind trust is not acceptable.
- Believe that if you give trust you will receive trust back.

SUBHA BARRY
INDIA

President of Working Mother Media

———◆———

Growing up in India as a Brahman, a member of the highest caste, I enjoyed a lot of privilege which served me well when I came to this country as a 20-year-old. Because I grew up as a member of the majority population, I was very self-confident and so was not aware that people were talking down to me or that they were putting me down because of my appearance or my accent. I think that growing up as part of a majority population gives you a self-confidence that stays with you even in a new country where you are now seen as a minority.

As a Hindu, Karma, that the good you do comes back to you and the bad that you do also comes back to you, plays a huge role in my belief system. Along with that also comes a belief that there is enough goodness in the world around us and if you are a good person that goodness will find its way to you. So, I tie these two things up, believing that there is enough goodness in the world and I continue to do the right thing as often as I can, because I think they have played a role in both my evolution as a leader and also in the success that I have found in this country.

That, in my opinion, is a basis for trust; trusting not only in friends, in your community, in your workplace, but really trusting the world around you in a way that says to you, I can only be counted for my actions, my behaviors, and I have to trust that that will be rewarded. With that kind of approach, I never lost that sense of trust about the world around me.

All the credit for that way of living can be credited to my religious and spiritual upbringing.

When I arrived in the United States, I earned two degrees in two years. I completed a Master's in Business Administration and a Masters in Accounting. I went on to become a commodities trader, then a wealth advisor, built a multicultural business development unit and then became the global head of diversity and inclusion at Merrill. There were a couple of other things that happened along the way that again, point to why I have so much faith and trust in the world around me. I've had enormous health issues along the way. I am a six-time cancer survivor. I have had five bouts with Hodgkin's lymphoma and one with breast cancer. Through each one of those journeys, somewhere somehow, that trust that you have inside of you and in people around you gets affirmed. Trust and gratitude for your family, your friends, your company, your colleagues, and for God is everything that enables you to make it through. With trust you are able to face whatever comes at you and without it the journey is most difficult.

The two things I would ask someone I was mentoring who just came to this country as an immigrant working in an organization that needs to grow are as follows:

1. How trustworthy are you?
2. What are you doing to be able to trust others?

You can change how you trust because, very often this notion of being able to trust somebody or not trust somebody often originates from your own head. You have to stand out as someone who is both trustworthy and somebody who is able to trust themselves. Both of those things actually spring out of a sense of confidence. Confidence in yourself and confidence in the world around you.

I recall a very painful experience that I am still processing. After achieving a great deal of success as a wealth advisor -I partnered with a marketer to build a diversity and inclusion initiative. She later turned against me and surreptitiously engaged in untrustworthy behavior that led to my firing and her replacing me. I was deeply hurt and devastated by this break of trust and betrayal.

In retrospect, several years later, I had three questions for myself, "had I done everything in my power to consider all the perspectives? Was I right to have dug in to defend my perspective?" and what could I have done differently or better in that situation?

I could have taken an alternative approach; I could have sat down on their side of the table to better understand their issues/their perspectives. It took me a long time to come to this realization that I could have done things differently. It has been almost ten years after my firing and re-hiring that I have really taken the time to go inside myself to ask, "What could I have done differently instead of just having stood up against it?" When trust is broken we question why that happened? They simply did something for themselves and I was in the way, collateral damage. Remember, you cannot control what someone else does, you can only control your reaction and response.

GEMS IN ACTION

Sanian Bailey

---◆---

Jackie Glenn is able to understand the feelings of others. Anytime I or a fellow intern would face conflict; she would always empathize with us. She would put herself in our shoes and navigate in the right direction when resolving the conflict. Most times she can relate because she went through the same thing or even worst. No matter what obstacles came her way she was able to overcome and conquer. Whether it be a conflict in her personal life or professional life; she is always able to recover quickly and keep pushing. She rarely complains but she puts a plan together and/ or prays about it.

She always has a positive outlook on everything. I recently just graduated from college and Jackie Glenn encouraged me to be resilient and to focus on the positive. She knew I was feeling down and always checked on me to make sure I was being resilient and being positive. She even went as far as connecting me with her colleagues. Her prayers, encouragement, and empathy have really helped me so I can help others. Just hearing stories from family, friends, and colleagues I can truly say Jackie Glenn is a God-Loving resilient woman who demonstrates empathy!"

Shani Bird

When I think of Mrs. Glenn, the first word that comes to my mind is authenticity. Not only does she demonstrate this attribute in her work every day, but she also displays this characteristic with the employees she has developed. I had the pleasure of working for Mrs. Glenn for a total of three years, and I saw her fondly as my "Work Mom." I knew that whenever I would walk through her office door, I would have a safe space where she would be both 100% authentic with me, and also truly committed to seeing me thrive in my role.

If I did a great job, she would almost shout from the roof tops about how fantastic a job I did; and if I had opportunities to improve, she would infuse humor and warmth – like a mother—and would say, "Come on, Shani, I know you can do this! Try again." I always knew where I stood with Mrs. Glenn and that is a quality you would be hard pressed to find in Corporate America. The impact she has made on my career, and the success I enjoy today, is immeasurable."

Yogita Inamdar

I am originally from India and moved to the United States almost 10 years ago. As an immigrant I consider myself as being part of the melting pot here in the United States. I have been on my own journey of understanding diversity and inclusion as I was trying to relate to my new-found identity as a minority and a woman of color.

I had the opportunity to meet Jackie Glenn for one of my MBA projects where I was interviewing senior D&I leaders to hear their best practices. At that time, she was a Global Chief Diversity Officer and was playing a key role in supporting programs and initiatives. She worked closely with the CEO who was committed to making the organization more inclusive.

During those conversations she came across as a very authentic and empathetic leader. She mentioned several programs and initiatives, but the one that resonated the most with me was her focus to design and implement diversity strategies to achieve inclusion within the organization and the role of emotional intelligence for leaders.

After that interview she and I stayed in touch. A job became available and she demonstrated her trademark empathy. I did not have a car at that time and was trying to be creative to get to the interview. Jackie changed the interview location to make it more convenient for me. This act of kindness and understanding motivated me to go above and beyond; to make sure that if I got a job on her team I will give more than my 100 percent as an employee because I would have such an accommodating manager who would respect me for who I am.

I can state numerous examples of her demonstrating empathy. One of the recent ones is when I was pregnant. She made sure that she accommodated my needs such as working from home and leaving for doctor's appointments. To ensure that my journey towards motherhood was very comfortable I worked from home during my last trimester which was a blessing.

Jackie went above and beyond to create more of a family kind of culture for the entire team and not just for me because I have seen it with other team members. I have yet to see a C-Suite executive who cooks for her team! I still rave about her black bean soup.

She has been very mindful and very aware of the work life balances working women and men have to deal with and she has made adjustments for all of us.

Trinidad Hermida

I had the pleasure of working with Jackie Glenn for almost four years as a Diversity and Inclusion Program Manager. Jackie has genuine concern and commitment for developing others. When I think about her, the first word that pops up is passion. She is passionate about life, diversity, inclusion and people. Her mantra; Lift as we climb. I am a recipient of this. My journey in corporate America began with Jackie. Even though I was her Executive Assistant at the time, she recognized I needed guidance, coaching and mentorship.

Jackie helped navigate me through a variety of transitions. One in particular was helping me to understand the impact of self-awareness. I wasn't aware of how I was being perceived by my colleagues. My style of communication was often misunderstood and considered offensive. Jackie took the time to coach me in appearance, demeanor and personal excellence. The conversations made me uncomfortable but I was willing to do what she suggested because I felt her genuine concern for who I was becoming. I don't know very many bosses that would take the time to develop their employees to the extent that Jackie did. It's because of her that I am pursuing my passion and making an impact in Diversity and Inclusion. I look forward to the day that I become someone else's Jackie.

Shayla Reed

I attended a conference and there was a panel that consisted of Jackie, another woman of color, an Indian and a white woman. The topic was overcoming Imposter Syndrome to become an authentic leader. The white woman spoke about coming from a background working primarily with men, an environment where she felt like she did not have to focus on imposter syndrome. She states that she could just show up and be herself and people would accept her. She even felt like she spoke for all women and she said that every woman should feel like this. I recalled Jackie in that moment reminding this woman of her white privilege. When the majority of the men in the room are of your race, there is a sense of comfort and belonging and there is no fear to be yourself.

Jackie then shared her story about being a black woman with an accent, working in a predominantly white environment. A culture where people bring their implicit bias with them everywhere they go. She shared and talked about how the more she began to embrace who she is, the better she did and the more others embraced her too. I have always found Jackie to be strong, extremely smart and supportive. In that moment she demonstrated her boldness to speak up to this woman on a panel in a room front of almost 500 people. She did this in such a way of grace and elegance, showing the audience that not only gender, but race matters. There are so many racial issues in this country, but it is important to embrace who you are. Jackie's action gave me confirmation that I need to show up and be my authentic self in every way possible and I love that about Jackie.

Catherine Okite

Your Best Self is not static –There are three criteria to being your best self. You must be making use of your strengths. You must be doing so in a way that has a constructive impact on others. It must be a positive experience for you. If you are using your strengths and others are benefiting, but you are miserable, you are not at your best. If you are enjoying yourself, but you are having a negative impact or no impact on others, you are not at your best. In order to truly manifest your best self, all three conditions must be in operation.

Jackie brought the best out of everyone. She is a dynamic and authentic leader. She had a positive impact and influence on everyone and as a result of her leadership, we grew as an organization and in our careers. She engaged with employees at all levels in the company and forged strategic partnerships in the community that help drive diversity and inclusion in the company. We all felt comfortable reaching out to Jackie and partnering with her on various diversity initiative. Jackie is the type of leader we should all strive to be.

Timothy Davidson
Communications Advisor

Working with Jackie at a large multinational corporation, I learned that trust is the fuel that powers her engine of inclusion. She is skilled at bringing together many different individuals and teams because she works diligently and respectfully to earn their trust. Through her conversations and candor, she helps even the most reserved people feel comfortable expressing areas where they want to improve or develop better understanding. She has an ability to help people be heard, and to realize that their voices matter. When they are not able to be present, she is trusted to represent them.

Jackie realizes that earning trust requires an investment. She gives hours of her time to hold conversations with people all over the world, from Board members to assembly workers, always seeking to understand. Perhaps the clearest expression of trust I have seen is with the men and women who have sought Jackie out as a mentor and guide for their own journeys. Whether she is advising someone professionally or personally, she helps people discover their strengths and develop their talents, and in the process she gives them the most valuable gift of all – learning to trust themselves."

CALL TO ACTION

In today's society, being an immigrant carries a stigma and there are many misconceptions regarding the policies, laws and regulations regarding immigrants and their status in America. The negative reputation of an immigrant colors the perception of many and makes accomplishing goals difficult. As an immigrant Black woman working in corporate America, I had to research and develop strategies to help me navigate the landscape while becoming a successful executive. This book will be a keepsake and a reference manual you will find yourself using over and over again. ENJOY!

ADDITIONAL RESOURCES ON IMMIGRATION & IMMIGRANTS

Granados, Samuel, "How Today's Visa Restrictions Might Impact Tomorrow's America," The Washington Post, February 21, 2017, available at:

https://www.washingtonpost.com/graphics/national/visas-impact/, accessed March 10, 2017, p.11. 65

Hunt, Jennifer, and Marjolaine Gauthier-Loiselle, "How Much Does Immigration Boost Innovation?," American Economic Journal: Macroeconomics, vol. 2, no. 2, 2010, pp. 31–56, available at: www.jstor.org/stable/25760296, accessed March 5, 2017, p. 37. This is based on data from the 2003 National Survey of College Graduates

"Immigrant CEOs of the Fortune 500," Boardroom Insiders, 2016, available at http://info.boardroominsiders.com/get-ourfortune-500-immigrant-ceo-list-for-free, accessed February 22, 2017.

Stangler, Dane and Jason Wiens, "The Economic Case for Welcoming Immigrant Entrepreneurs," The Kauffman Foundation, September 8, 2015, available at http://www.kauffman.org/what-we-do/resources/entrepreneurship-policy-digest/theeconomic-case-for-welcoming-immigrant-entrepreneurs, accessed March 7, 2017.

NOTES

[1]Molinsky, Andy. Everyone Suffers from Imposter Syndrome-Here's How to Handle It. *Harvard Business Review, July 7, 2016.* Retrieved from http://hbr.org/2016/07/everyone-suffers-from-imposter-syndrome-here's-how-to-handle-it

[2]Sakuiku, J. September 2011. The Imposter Phenomenon. *The International Journal of Behavioral Science.* 75-97. Retrieved from https://doi.org/10.14456/ijbs.2011.6

[3]Luke 1:28 NIV

[4]Ibid

[5]2 Timothy 1:7 KJV.

[6]Philippians 4:13 NIV.

[7] Saint Francis of Assisi. "For it is in Giving that We Receive." Retrieved from https://www.google.com

[8]Google Dictionary. Retrieved from https://www.google.com/search?=google.dictionary

[9]Ibid

[10]Jackson, Mahalia. If I Can Help Somebody. Retrieved from https://www.lyricsfreak.com/m/mahalia+jackson/if+i+can+help+somebody_205986

[11]Shakespeare, William. Hamlet (Act 1. Scene III). Retrieved from https://literarydevices.net/to-thine-own-self-be-true

[12]Psalm 75:6-7

[13] Angelou, Maya. "When people show you who they are, believe them (the first time)." Retrieved from https://www.goodreads.com/quotes/518149-when-people-show-you-who-they-are-believe-them-the-first-time

JACKIE GLENN

Global Diversity & Inclusion
Executive & Consultant

A pioneering Diversity and Inclusion expert Jackie Glenn lives by the mantra, "It's better to be respected than liked." Her groundbreaking initiatives have reshaped organizational policies, unified a multidimensional corporate culture, and generated international interest and intrigue. By solidifying business relationships, securing overwhelming buy-in and offering a wealth of information, Jackie was pivotal in guiding Fortune 500 EMC Corporation to personify its brand of innovation in the global community.

As an engaging public speaker, Jackie begins every presentation with "Hi, I'm Jackie Glenn and I hail from the island of Jamaica!" This simply showcases that Jackie mirrors the behavior she expects – authenticity and confidence as defined by experience. Her zest for life and commitment to excellence has manifested itself by creating a corporate environment that embodies inclusivity, energy, and a mentality for change and growth.

Jackie joined EMC Corporation in 2000 and quickly progressed to Senior Director of HR Operations for a global salesforce of more than 2000. In this role she conceived, planned, and developed programs in organizational development, leadership consulting, employee training and development. She is known for her ability to recognize high-potential talent and as such individual coaching and mentoring became a key resource for those who wanted to raise their game.

Jackie's leadership as Global Chief Diversity Officer resulted in a number of industry-recognized best practices. She created a groundbreaking transgender reassignment and benefits program, multiple women's corporate advancement immersion experiences, and recruiting partnerships with Historically Black Colleges and Universities (HBCUs) that feature a summer internship and build a pipeline of high-potential future employees in the STEM field. She introduced corporate-wide affinity circles that acknowledge the power of influence when like-minded individuals join forces.

These initiatives have resulted in various honors and press coverage for EMC including; DiversityInc who listed EMC as a *Top 25 Noteworthy Company,* Disability Matters named EMC a *Leading Employer* and a five year run with a perfect score on the *Human Rights Campaign Corporate Equality Index.*

Jackie has been awarded and acknowledged globally for her commitment to inclusivity and diversity. Some of them include *Champion of Diversity* (NY Urban League), *Founder's Award* (Lawyer's Committee for Civil Rights & Economic Justice, *Black History Leadership* (Whittier Street), *Boston's 100 Most Influential People* (Get Konnected!), *Top 10 Influential Women in Diversity* (Diversity Global Magazine),and *Women of Excellence/ Global Women's Champion* (National Association for Female Executives).

Jackie holds a Master of Science degree in Human Resources Management from Lesley University, Cambridge, MA and a bachelor's degree from Emmanuel College, Boston. Her love for community advocacy and civic leadership includes service on the Board of the Children's Services of Roxbury (MA), the Board of the African-American Museum of Boston, and the Board of Overseers of Beth Israel Deaconess Hospital.

A world traveler, she frequently hosts national and international conferences, participates on industry panels, and addresses groups on what she knows best – diversity and inclusion in the workplace, advancement of women in technology, transgender reassignment, and living a fulfilled life.

Jackie can be reached @ § glennjackie3@gmail.com § LinkedIn Profile